*"The anatomies of my chosen surroundings
are rich with meaning . . . and are a snapshot
(or many snapshots) of a lifetime spent
in the world of design."*

Alexa Hampton takes you on a tour through her evolving life
in design, attested by the countless updates and redecorations
of her own home, a beautifully appointed prewar apartment on
Manhattan's Upper East Side, and the art, textiles, and objects
that she's collected and treasured over the years. Throughout
the book, Alexa reminisces about the design and style luminaries
who have inspired her interiors, including the work of legendary
interior designer David Hicks, a mentor of Alexa's father, Mark,
whose deft use of rich and saturated colors encouraged Alexa's
own love of pinks and purples. She reflects on her friend and
fashion designer Bill Blass's gutsy restraint and unerring good
taste in creating his well-manicured home. Along the way, she
also explores some of the key moments that rocked the world of
design—including Christie's 1993 sale of celebrated couturier
Hubert de Givenchy's estate—and how they made an indelible
mark on her.

An intimate look into Alexa's understanding of influence that
will get you inside the head of a distinguished designer, *Alexa
Hampton: Design, Style & Influence* is not only a personal history
of interior design, but also a love letter to what she believes any
home should be for its owner.

ALEXA
HAMPTON

ALEXA HAMPTON

DESIGN, STYLE & INFLUENCE

ALEXA HAMPTON WITH ROSY NGO

PRINCIPAL PHOTOGRAPHY BY STEVE FREIHON

CLARKSON POTTER/PUBLISHERS
NEW YORK

I started working in my father's office (photographed here in 2014) when I was thirteen, in bursts, but he and my mother began exposing me to the language of design well before then.

For Barbara Geisha Hamilton Dauphin-Duthuit, with love for a lifetime of friendship, and for my family and colleagues.

MARK
HAMPTON
LLC

ALEXA
HAMPTON
INC.

CONTENTS

HOW I GOT HERE

AS THE DAUGHTER of a famous and beloved decorator,* I have often been asked when I knew I wanted to go into the very business that my father, Mark Hampton, helped pioneer alongside many greats such as David Hicks, Sister Parish, Albert Hadley, Mario Buatta, and the like, all of whom most shaped the profession into what it resembles today. As I have answered this question so many times in just the same way over many, many years, I will put it down, here and now, in writing, so I can easily refer to this as my official printed response.

Like many people who thrive in New York City, my parents, having grown up elsewhere, were not that rare breed of native-born New Yorkers. They met, married, and moved there together as recent college graduates. My father, like many cool cats before him, hailed from Indiana (see Halston, Bill Blass, and Cole Porter). My mother, Duane Flegel, had a more circuitous path. She was born in Portland, Oregon, spent a year in Thailand, and then came back to the United States to settle in Pennsylvania for her high school years. She and my father began courting after meeting in Europe one summer during college, and when they finally arrived as a couple in New York, they each attended graduate school to attain their master's degrees—he in northern Renaissance art, and she in English.

Not-so-fun fact: I am the only person in my immediate family without a graduate degree. I gave up my graduate career after a year at my father's illustrious alma mater: New York University's Institute of Fine Arts. I have since had the extreme honor of receiving two honorary PhDs, one from the Moore College of Art and Design in Philadelphia and the other from the New York School of Interior Design. (My joke is that I have twice the degrees but half the knowledge. I am not sure if I am actually amused by this.)

New York, to my mind, is for those who will take it. As with many working professionals (and I bet all those who are "children of"), I have often experienced imposter syndrome. Does it count that I was born here? Does it count that I came up through the ranks of a company owned by my father? Does it count as success, given that I bear his last name? It is all impossible to answer and surely not worth the breath to ask. As the Magic 8 Ball tells us, "Reply hazy, try again." But, as youngsters, we all think that the world will be our oyster. What isn't in our grasp? Ah, the folly and arrogance of youth.

As all the studies confirm, American children score highest in confidence and not much else. To my child's mind, my parents' life seemed thrilling (and it

---

*Mark Hampton's definition of *decorator* versus *designer*: When you are painting rooms, buying carpets, and installing curtains, you are decorating. When you are adding a room, selecting crown moldings, and the like, you are designing. Take it or leave it.

OVERLEAF, TOP AND BOTTOM: In 1998, I became president and owner of my father's iconic firm; then in 2000, I established Alexa Hampton, Inc., a separate, yet complementary, business-to-house product collaborations.

OPPOSITE: A Roman bust on top of a William Kent table flanked by a pair of beehive planters anchored first my father's private office and then mine. The photograph of my father and me was taken in a photobooth after we saw *Terminator 2*. All my best photos with him are of the photobooth variety.

was). Hard work during the day, fancy parties at night, and glamorous trips to beautiful places seemed just the thing. I was born, and remain, an extreme extrovert. I confidently wanted to crash all of my parents' parties and be included in all their trips. Their friends were so much fun! There was always room at the table for my sister and me and, for the most part, it could be terribly entertaining to be there. (I will not get into too much detail about the time we were served oeuf en gelée at Lee Radziwill's—yes, the princess and younger sister of Jacqueline Kennedy Onassis—but I will tell you that my father pinching me hard under the table let it be known that I would have to eat that disgusting, congealed witches' brew and that there would be no escape. So, there were definitely moments of resistance if not out-right defiance. At least I also got to sneak downstairs to the TV room that particular weekend, where her patient son Anthony let me watch my first *Saturday Night Live* episode with him. I was somewhere between eight and ten, and he was a saint in his twenties. I remember think-ing the Coneheads were ridiculous.)

I could draw at an early age, and I decided that, well, if my father can draw and I can draw, surely I should look toward him as an example for my future. Right? I mean the similarities were obvious (they were not). So, when I hit thirteen, I began working in his office for a few weeks that summer. What did this mean, you might ask? In the beginning, I would read romance novels at the front desk and answer calls. I imagine I presented to my father's long-suffering colleagues as a hideous facsimile of Eloise trying to regale the staff of the Plaza, and they had to endure it. But I persisted in showing my genuine interest in interior decorating, and I kept coming back each sum-mer. I'd go to the fabled Decoration & Design Building, home to most of the New York City fabric houses open only to the trade, to return or pick up samples for the decorators. Eventually, I was allowed to shop for them as my list of responsibilities grew.

Somewhere during this time, my mother and her friend Louise Grunwald (then Melhado) opened an antiques shop called MH Stockroom. Their Aladdin's cave in that tiny, by-appointment-only space was beyond wonderful to visit. Even better, they replenished their store during shopping trips abroad (*mon dieu!*). Between MH Stockroom and Niall Smith Antiques on Bleecker Street, my passion for souvenirs from the grand tour (an eighteenth- and nineteenth-century rite-of-passage trip that many aristocratic English college graduates took to the Continent to round out their education in classical art, history, and culture) was cemented for all time.

However, it was really when I was not in the office that the work of influence was wending its way through me. My academically minded parents wanted to tour houses and museums and galleries, ad nauseam, quite literally. (In my first book, I mentioned throwing up at Giverny, but I also threw up at Harry's Bar in Florence, all over their dining room. I threw up all over the English countryside. I threw up in Tuscany. I threw up traveling through India. I even threw up once in my father's face as he begged me to try to wait to get upstairs to our apart-ment's bathroom.) In between all this dyspepsia, how-ever, we were actually making it to all those museums and houses and antiques stores. What began as torture, boredom, and illness turned into fun, and, eventually, I was hooked.

These days, as a parent, I realize now that what my parents were doing then was teaching me and my sister a second language, a visual language by which to see and register good design. They kept speaking often and at great length in that language until we became fluent. Period. The museum-going was an obvious tactic, but an insidious campaign as well. Our exposure to the dwell-ings of interesting tastemakers, architects, doyennes, writers, and others was frequently wrapped up in happy occasions. Beauty came with Christmas. The Uffizi Gallery in Florence was smuggled in under the cover of gelato. And this is how my influences came to take root, and I am grateful for it.

_____

OPPOSITE: For about thirty years, this hallway guided our firm's clients to the principal's office, where I was from 1998 to 2021.

OVERLEAF: This iteration of my dining room delivers Pavlos's wishes when we expanded the apartment's footprint for the second time: a green dining room and maps. Both provide the perfect accompaniment for the classical elements that make up the rest of the decor, all sober and dignified when not in service to gluttony.

INFLUENCE AND LOVE

GREAT MEMORIES have a sensory response that accompanies them. We all know and are perhaps tired of hearing about Proust's madeleine, as its story is so oft-repeated, but it has become such a cliché only because it rings so true. Taste and memory are forever connected. For me, though, despite the fact that I simply adore eating, my most cherished memories have combined and attached themselves forever to my other kind of taste—my visual taste.

Like a chef who sits around dreaming about what their perfect last meal might be, when I think of my last supper, I see frescoes and Da Vinci (frequently) and Italy and its churches (always). My taste buds delight in moments of the "exotic" (which could encompass almost anything to an American child born in the 1970s), weaving together rich dark brown paint, animal prints, bleached columns connoting neoclassical buildings big and, especially, small (architectural models being just so amazing), trompe l'oeil, and bivouacs. There is a lot of pastiche, a visual Bohemian rhapsody of mixing and remixing, much like Queen's mashup of musical genres in their iconic song.

I respectfully borrow many of the tics and talismans of my heroes as a nod to their importance in my life and in an attempt to reap the sensory gratification that they have conferred upon me. These taste heroes include my parents, friends, personalities that have loomed large in my life, interior design contemporaries, and, of course, the big decorative moments and seismic shifts with which anyone growing up in the design world of the 1990s, especially in my family, would be familiar. Together, the many influences behind my taste tell the story of who I am, where I've come from, where I've gone, and where I would like to go still as I live and contribute to the fantastic and endless world of design and style.

Nowhere is this style stew of semiotics more apparent than in my home in New York. What started with obvious salutations to design greats, like my father, Albert Hadley, and Bill Blass, has evolved as I have been exposed over time to the commissions taken by my firm, to travels around the world, and to the trips I've taken through the pages of magazines, as well as Pinterest, Instagram, and more. And more. And more. Things have been added and things have been taken away. In some areas, I have distilled what I like best (objects); while in other areas, I am still playing and discovering my views (color).

Having lived in the same building in New York City for the last twenty-seven years, I can see these twists and turns as they have occurred and been memorialized in print, like a map of my past and a diagram of where my head was at during my various stops on the stations of the decorative cross. I hope that by sharing this map with you, I can pay homage to those people who have given me such joy and inspiration through design. I am reminded of Flaubert, wherein he declares that the role of the author is to be "present everywhere, yet visible nowhere." Although, when it comes to influence and interior design, it is all expressed by what is visible.

OPPOSITE: My sofa at work was a great place to hang out. I much prefer lap work to desk work.

My private room at work had all my favorite things: bamboo blinds,
a William Kent table, a mahogany cellarette, a French desk, a
Christopher Spitzmiller lamp, and a Karl Springer conference table.

WHY THIS BUILDING?

NO MATTER HOW FAR and wide I go on this beautiful blue planet, I continue to return home to New York where I was born and raised. The grass is not necessarily greener on the other side when Manhattan is your home (albeit there's a lot more grass elsewhere). To put a finer point on it, I have never lived more than a few miles from my childhood home (except during college), and I have maintained the same street address since I was twenty-four.

After graduating from Brown University in Rhode Island and studying at NYU's Institute of Fine Arts in New York and Florence, Italy, I moved back home to the city to work as a decorator at my father's firm. I had hoped to live with my parents on Park Avenue to save money for my own rental, but my father's reply was, "Sorry, Sweetie, we already have an apartment for you. You can't come home. It would be far too disruptive for your mother." In my lifetime, I have not seen a better example of spousal devotion and self-preservation at the same time.

Too bad I hated the rental. After living in the apartment that my parents had arranged for me on Lexington Avenue until the yearlong lease was up, I bounced around Manhattan for a while. I dragged voluminous packing boxes back and forth from my boyfriend's place to my best friend Gaby's law-school dorm room (as she pretty much lived with her then boyfriend, now husband), depending on which level of High Drama my relationship occupied. Turns out that obsessively reading romance novels from the age of twelve well into my twenties—okay, thirties—is not good for a healthy

relationship. During one memorable battle, conducted in public (naturally), I screamed at my boyfriend accusatorially for being a drama queen. "Please," he said solemnly, a manly Spaniard to the end, "Drama *King*."

During this time, Gaby and I were looking for an apartment commensurate with our salaries. As I think I've hinted, she was a brilliant young legal brain and I, a young decorator, so we weren't exactly on even footing—my budget was much tighter than hers. We saw so many duds. We heard a lot about temporary interior walls. Who knew? We saw a Lower East Side walk-up that actually had a tub in the middle of the kitchen/living room. I had read about these in turn-of-the-century novels (those being the nineteenth to twentieth centuries). I had no idea such a thing was still even possible, and it was unwelcome information.

Sometimes one needs to leave behind the comforts of home to recognize the privileges and advantages of their upbringing. As my father was the son of an undertaker and grew up on a farm in Indiana, he and my mother took great pains to point out how lucky my sister and I were, but I don't think we could really appreciate the view from the catbird seats until we were jettisoned from them. Truly, youth is wasted on the young!

Finally, one day, Gaby found a listing in the *New York Times* for a two-bedroom apartment with two bathrooms, a kitchen, and a fireplace in the living room, all in a very convenient location. We immediately assumed it harbored roaches, ghosts, and a murderer squatting in a closet. We signed on the dotted line anyway. We could always call an exterminator.

And that is how I came to find this building, where I have lived in five different apartments on three different floors across three decades. Although I am a wannabe Park Avenue Princess by birth, I have ignominiously and surely permanently slid down to Midtown East. (Although I will still stubbornly claim it's the Upper East Side—facts be damned! But, I don't want to lie to you, dear reader.)

The truth of the matter was that this building was a mix of rentals and co-ops and on its way to converting entirely to a cooperatively owned building. I imagine that the management just didn't entirely have its act together yet, and that is how Gaby and I came to live in the very place to which I have become so attached. So, there the stage is set for what is to come.

ABOVE: This silver hand-painted Gracie wallpaper served my family well in the entryway for more than a decade. Its shimmery background lent a glow to the apartment's only room without natural light.

ABOVE: I'm not sure when I became obsessed with lion imagery, but my mother gave me this winged lion–bedecked crest, I knew exactly where it would go: in the passageway from the living room to our principal bedroom of my forever home.

RIGHT: The family room in its 2015 incarnation is the granddaddy of all the rooms. Knowing I would have a monochromatic montage of art drove me to pick a color for the walls that would amplify the collected heliogravures by d'Espousy.

CHAPTER 1

DISCOVERING
12C

I AM A NEW YORKER—BORN and will ever be. Gaby and I were both eight years old when we first met. It was the late 1970s, and she was kitted up in a ballerina tutu, leotard, and toe shoes while I was wearing a sequined top, short shorts, and roller skates. An epic battle of Greasers versus Socials, à la *The Outsiders*, did not ensue on Park Avenue when we encountered one another. Instead, Gaby and I became fast friends and have remained close many decades later. We attended the same high school, visited each other in college, and were in each other's weddings. As only two weirdos would do, we decided to have babies at the same time. I knew she was pregnant before her husband did, and her daughter and my twin sons were born ten days apart. If that's not a committed relationship, I don't know what is.

So, when Gaby and I signed the lease for 12C, a two-bedroom apartment in a very central location, we were ecstatic. Sure, signing your first lease is a huge milestone for every twentysomething, but the elation that she and I felt after searching high and low was nothing short of euphoric. Finding a decent and affordable apartment in

New York City can be challenging in the best of times with the full might of technology and high-speed internet, but this was 1995, an era when fax machines were far more common than internet connections (dial-up, no less) and then only in business environments.

Trudging throughout the city—uptown and downtown, east side and west side—in search of something that didn't scare our parents but could fit our budgets oftentimes felt as if we were looking for the Holy Grail. Finding the listing for 12C the old-fashioned way in the paper of record (does anyone else remember classified ads?) and then securing an actually beautiful two-bedroom apartment with two bathrooms in a gorgeous prewar building with a doorman in a great neighborhood felt like we had just been awarded genius grants from the MacArthur Fellows.

OPPOSITE: New York's skyline, like the city itself, is always dynamic and awe-inspiring. Though the skyline has changed, sometimes dramatically, even in my lifetime, one thing remains constant: I will always love it and never tire of the potential the city holds.

BACHELORETTE
LIVING

We were living the dream as scrappy twentysomething New Yorkers, but no one would ever know that by judging the interiors of the apartment. Legendary fashion photographer Arthur Elgort shot me in my apartment for the February 1996 issue of *Vogue*, and the writer seemed perplexed that one so young could love and live with so many classical design elements. Then, just as now, grand tour souvenirs, marble busts, and finely made furniture beguiled me, so those were the objects prominently placed. Gaby and I furnished the apartment with a few pieces from my father's storeroom of various samples and leftovers from other projects. We were grateful for anything and everything.

A fresh coat of paint would really make the apartment feel like it was uniquely ours, so I set out to paint it with custom colors, mixed by moi. Almost periwinkle in hue, French matting–type blue walls would give the room the right touch, I thought. I painted a coat and then gave it a second, hoping the additional layer would dry, yielding the velvety richness I had imagined in my mind's eye. That didn't do the trick, so I stirred in more black. And more. And again with the black paint until the color was just right.

Happy with the living room, I moved on to my bedroom. I stayed up all night painting it yellow, but the rising sun illuminated the catastrophe before me. In the light of day, I realized I had mixed the perfect shade of insanity. Yellow is famous for being the hardest color to get right, and I have found that to be true. I cut the color 50 percent with white and then put down my paintbrushes.

RIGHT: After trying out a few settings post-college, when I seldom bothered to unpack my moving boxes because I knew I'd be elsewhere soon enough, it felt really, really, really good to stretch out a bit and be in a place where I wanted to stay surrounded by things I love. Never a fan of unpacking—suitcases, groceries, moving boxes, you name it, I hate it—I basked in the idea of unwrapping and displaying my beloved obelisks, framed family photos, and drawings; bathed in the bright sunlight streaming through the gorgeous casement windows trimmed in white.

GROWING UP HAMPTON:
PARK AVENUE

In 1971, before a certain blessed event, my parents moved into the apartment where my mother still lives. I refer to this fact to explain that I was raised in one single place. My parents were lucky enough to find their forever home, entirely intact, while they were young, and there they stayed put. I, too, am sticky in this way. I like to find a place and dig in. I am a double Taurus after all, dear reader. When I am not charging at the world, I am supine and munching on something.

As a very social child, I went to many friends' houses for hangouts and overnights, though I always preferred having people come to visit my house (as New Yorkers persist in calling their apartments, just like we say "the country" when we mean anywhere outside of the city. It's weird, but it's our thing, nonetheless). I wanted to stay in my apartment because it was home, but also because I found it beautiful. My surroundings have always had a huge impact on me and my sense of happiness, and I loved and still love my parents' apartment.

I think that my father was particularly gifted in his creation of furniture plans, having studied those of the greats who preceded him. David Hicks and Albert Hadley were able to harness and refine my father's nascent gifts when he was still in the very earliest part of his career, and he, in turn, passed his knowledge along to his staff, loving this very act of impartation.* He shared and demonstrated his talents to all who worked at MHLLC (née Mark Hampton, Inc.). Everyone that I know who has come out of the office appreciates the critical importance of a good solid floor plan. The only thing better is one that has some leeway to be adjusted for entertainment. The floor plan is the map of any room, and it is entirely apparent when "X" does not mark the spot.

As a designer who has lived in a single space for more than three decades, I also observed that the logic of a space can be found, identified, and reinvested with meaning many times over without ever needing to abandon

it. The basic furniture placement in the apartment has been altered very little, if at all, since 1971; however, the look changed radically in the thirty years that my father lived there. In the 1970s, for example, the living room was a deep ox-blood red and featured a black-tar painting on the wall, plastic tables, David Hicks fabrics, an antique area rug, and dark red curtains.

In the 1980s, Mark waved his magic wand again and it became an English (emphasis on the *ish*) country-house interior. Inspired to correspond in some fashion with the neo-Georgian architecture of many prewar New York apartments, these country-house rooms were strangely successful, lining each side of the city's streets. Colefax and Fowler's structured cabbage-rose chintz was upholstered upon the walls and flowed directly into the tableau curtains. Once so sheathed, the living room was populated by a Victorian desk, French open-armchairs, Edwardian upholstery, and a pair of black-framed Napoleon III low chairs flanking the mantel. Everything that was not covered in the chintz (and most things were) harmonized with it by picking up the colors present in the pattern. The result was a soothing experience for an otherwise technically busy room. But the furniture plan remained almost identical to its 1970s incarnation.

As the late 1980s arrived, the chintz, ever discreet, exited stage right. The oh-so-country-ness of the living room was left in favor of total visual structure, though not stricture. Everything was tan, cream, and white chastity—a bold move considering the teenager in residence (I think my sister had already left for college by this point). Columns were erected, pilasters were placed, and I felt my parents' choices for their most used room reflected their assumption of irrefutable adulthood. Draping it in maturity, like a mantle, my parents had aged into being more serious people. The room wasn't pedigreed or stuffy; it simply expressed the preferences of a couple who knew who they were and how they wanted

---

OPPOSITE: As my parents matured, their decor did too. The once-black entry hall was painted with faux-marble panel design and eighteenth-century chairs bookend a Regency cabinet.

to live. The furniture placement had moved not one iota from the prior chintz years—although the Victorian bamboo desk had been put out to pasture in the country sometime before.

For us all, this meant that despite the radical changes from one decade to the next, we, the inhabitants of the apartment, never felt alienated by style's evolution. Function was never ceded to reinvent the sensibility of the apartment. In the dark of night, stumbling to the kitchen microwave to make a Stouffer's French bread pizza, I would never need to redirect my path to know where I was heading. That is, in part, central to what makes a house a home.

There is much more I could say about this apartment that I love, but I will let the photos do the talking.

ABOVE: The Coromandel folding screen has been in my family for as long as I remember, having originally belonged to my maternal grandmother. I love how the red in the lacquerware and books hint at what's to come in the dining room.

OPPOSITE: The tall mirrored folding screen used to have a twin until an unfortunate mishap involving a certain enthusiastic eight-year-old birthday girl chasing a handsome magician caused its destruction. That incident didn't deter me from getting a pair to use in my own home as an adult.

OPPOSITE: In the dining room, cornice and baseboards were marbleized to anchor the oxblood-red paneled walls. In front of the Venetian mirror sits a bronze of my sister Kate by artist George "Fowokan" Kelly in between two green malachite obelisks and a collection of crystal decanters.

ABOVE: One of a pair, this gilded neoclassical side table with a Roman white urn sits in the dining room of my childhood apartment on Park Avenue where my mother still lives.

Having ample seating is paramount for a living room's function. A solid floor plan will account for movable chairs to accommodate more guests. The low Chinese coffee table has been in service since the room was bathed in chintz.

ABOVE: Duane's Gothic side chairs flank an English secretary with a Louis XVI open-arm chair. My mother's obsessive love of family photos has effectively guaranteed their virtual absence in my apartment.

RIGHT: Celadon is a celebrated color, once reserved only for ancient Chinese royalty. When paired with shagreen, as it is in an antique eyeglass case, magnifying glass, and box, the combination is a downright delicious potpourri.

Bigger is not necessarily better when it comes to decorating. I love how Mark played with scale in the living room: pairing the hovering bookcases and vertical lines of the walls against the low Napoleon III chairs flanking the fireplace.

ABOVE: The books with lighter jackets are arranged in the bookcase closest to the window so that the natural bleaching that occurs with light isn't noticeable, while the books with darker covers are kept further away from the window. While not one to shelve his books by color, my father did want them safe.

LEFT: Brown, beige, and white–striped upholstery is a nice juxtaposition to the curved back on the overstuffed bustle-back armchair, the rolled arms of the tufted Carr sofa, and the graceful lines of the *en tableau* curtains.

OPPOSITE, CLOCKWISE FROM TOP LEFT: Duane's red lacquerware collection in the foreground reminds her of youth in Thailand, while the red marble tabletop (supporting a statue of St. Paul) delivers more color.

On the left living room bookcase, as in ancient Rome and now the contemporary Hampton home, porphyry vases are greatly cherished. Unlike granite, this volcanic stone has flecks of clear feldspar crystal throughout the rest of the dark reddish purple. David Hicks certainly helped lead the Hamptons on this path.

The light beige-painted stripes on the walls add to the trompe l'oeil faux bois painting and celadon collection to create a moment of poetic harmony. Every time I look at this vignette, I am struck by its beauty—not bad for a thirty-five-year-old room.

Assorted paintings of my parents hang above a collection of marble, porcelain statues, obelisks, and miniatures. My mother loves giraffes and her devotion to them appears throughout the apartment. Recently, for her birthday, I took her to the zoo for a private encounter with the stately creature.

HAMPTONS IN SOUTHAMPTON

In the early 1980s, a dear family friend enlisted my father to help spruce up a gardener's cottage on his property, thinking that it might be a good place to rent out. He was not wrong. My father eventually purchased the house, added a double cube–size living room and a new main bedroom suite, planted a garden, put French doors on the garage, and rechristened it the Pool House. In the summer of 1983, in we moved, with my parents parking their pendant wood-sided station wagons snugly in the driveway.

This was the house where I would shutter my teenage self in my upstairs room on winter weekends and descend to grab food, only to reascend the stairs to retreat grumpily into my saturnine lair. My father vehemently resisted the idea of a television antenna on top of the house, as he deemed it an eyesore (likewise he vetoed a diving board), so that left us able only to read or watch VHS tapes in our free time (we were not known for our athleticism). The consequence was that my sister and I read a lot of books there and are, to this day, absolute experts in black-and-white classic movies, most musicals, and foreign films.

In the summertime, the house transformed. My parents entertained at least once a weekend, and we spent sun-kissed days at a beach club. Most spectacularly, it was the location for our annual keg party that my parents let my sister and me throw once a summer; starting, I think, when I was fifteen and Kate seventeen. My mother and father would go buy the beer for us, set up the stereo and keg, and then lock themselves in the house and hide upstairs, hoping for the best. It lasted only a few years before we moved on to nightclubs, but, boy, was it fun!

Christmas and Thanksgiving were frequently set against the backdrop of these rooms, and the house offered shelter to my family of five during the first year of

ABOVE AND OPPOSITE: As I learned the hard way when I painted my bedroom in 12C, it can be difficult to see how much pigment a color has when it isn't seen in context with the adjacent trim, usually white. When they are viewed together, a person can get a better sense of how bright the colors are. This is true for all soft tones, including apple green; as seen here in the entry hall of the Southampton house; they can read much stronger en masse and in context with trim. These colors should be attempted by only the most experienced as well as brave.

COVID-19. It already held great memories from many eras, but now it has renewed and reshaped sentimental value to our family post-pandemic.

At the same time that it was carving out meaning for me personally, this house marked a definitive decorating moment for those who are familiar with and fond of my father's work. I had the great honor of watching Mary McDonald tear up one night a few years ago after dinner, when she realized we were chilling in *that* room. Granted, wine had been imbibed, and Mary is obviously engaged in this wild world of design, but still. I have puffed up with great pride when showing people the living room of this little house, a room that I find endlessly current.

The absolutely counterintuitive idea to paint the living room walls a rich dark brown and to have crisp white millwork is pretty funny considering the fact that it is a house at the beach. What began littered with brown Brunschwig & Fils La Portugaise–covered upholstery (made famous by Brooke Astor's red-lacquered library)

ABOVE: Dark walls may not be evocative of breezy beach houses but there is none more perfectly decorated than this Southampton Hampton abode to my mind. The bitter-chocolate walls are cool and sophisticated while the sisal rug and linen-and-cotton slipcovered furniture keep things grounded and airy.

OPPOSITE, CLOCKWISE FROM TOP LEFT: A Roman bust on a fluted shaft, architectural models, and drawings, these are all elements that have seeped into my soul and make repeated appearances in my work.

A white architectural bookcase provides a graphic anchor for my parents' living room on Long Island. While its silhouette is classical, the lack of carved embellishments makes it a more modern presence.

The transition from apple green to dark brown as one moves from the entryway to the living room has always been satisfying for me. The geometric painted bookcase is grounded by fluted mahogany columns topped by Venus and Apollo.

Roman shades, and curtains on rings, keep the curtains as casual as the slipcovered furniture. The rolled arms on the Breck-style sofa make it a suitable spot for lazy summer naps.

ABOVE: "Traditional American design" seems oxymoronic to me because we are a proud country of mutts, and the notion of "American" design didn't exist prior to the last century. Instead of working to our detriment, it is our greatest liberty (design-related, that is) because of the inherent creative license to play with and combine things from other aesthetics and all style genres. Here, my father combined a neoclassical fireplace, a gilded Victorian mirror, and a pedimented bookshelf of his own design with an American country cross-stitched chest to good effect.

LEFT: Though I'm not one to love images of bathrooms, this one is different. It is a jewelbox papered with Pugin's *House of Parliament*.

OPPOSITE: A small copy of Pauline Borghese, Napoleon's sister, as Canova's Venus Victrix has prize of place on our living room center table.

Perhaps it was the way my father deftly mixed periods and styles that has made traditional American design so appealing to me. I love that its style comes together democratically and doesn't follow a top-down Victorian ethos.

RIGHT, TOP: Greige and white stripes are threaded throughout the house, tying together each room and its distinct color scheme.

RIGHT, BOTTOM: Blue-and-white rooms never seem out of place at the beach.

OPPOSITE: The greige-and-white-striped fabric from the living room is carried over into the dining room where it adorns chairs of my design for Hickory Chair. The chairs themselves are meant to evoke a plaster whimsy in the vein of Sirmos plaster but also an appreciation of trompe l'œil playfulness.

ended up slip-covered in a ruffled, white self-stripe. If anything, over time the house became less "country" on the inside but also fresher and less datable.

We used this house to its absolute limit during the initial COVID lockdown. Each of our three children needed a private classroom space, my husband required an office with a door, and I roamed the house, leaving a mess in my wake as I went from room to room, always to be pushed out by someone. I came to realize our pool-house game needed switching up with another room that's as fun to sit in as the living room. As I wondered what we should do, I thought it might be nice to have a room with a color scheme that would be compatible with the living room but still suitable for kids *and* adults. Since we had long ago installed a proper television with cable, and now Apple TV, this room would be used a lot. I put a dumpster in the driveway and went to work. (Thank heavens my mother never saw it.)

I used the Nobilis wood wallpaper for which they are famous (and of which I cannot get enough), and I made our bitty pool house equally *not* country but still in the whites and grays of the living room. In fact, the living room, dining room, and pool house all share a variety of gray and white stripes, and I have come to enjoy the fact that this small house is kept tight by sharing a common thread of color.

RIGHT: Our pool house (nee the garage) needed an update during COVID. I adapted what I had in my New York office to this space, replete with my favorite Nobilis wood-patterned wallpaper and white gesso table.

A model of the Milan cathedral, a driftwood coffee table, and Georges Braque prints decorate the pool house.

MARK HAMPTON WITH SUSAN AND CARTER BURDEN

As I mentioned earlier in this book, I find that influence is sometimes subversive. It is frequently ushered into one's consciousness through a Trojan horse. So has been my experience of the tastes of Susan and Carter Burden, two of my parents' very best friends. I grew up going to the Burdens. As a young child, that meant spending a good chunk of each summer as their guests in East Hampton. The younger Burdens, Belle and Carter, were and are like family to me. I have loved the entire bunch as long as I have drawn breath, and I expect to love them until the day I die. I can go long stretches without seeing them and yet be freshly gleeful the minute we are reunited, picking up where we left off, even if (ugh) years have passed in between.

When, as kids, we were told that we were going to the Burdens, I was always incredibly excited. Although I frequently preferred staying at our house over visiting someone else's, that was never the case with them. The Burdens were and are, in fact, the most fun of anyone. I had the best giggles with them. They had a pack of the cutest pugs you'll ever see. They had the best food. There were pinball machines. There were jars filled with candy and nuts and an arcade-size version of Centipede, for goodness' sake! It was a wonderland, one that came with the funniest and smartest and kindest of friends. And, this is the subversive part: All that fun and love and laughs happened in rooms of unparalleled beauty.

I never stood a chance of not loving the interiors that Susan and Carter created with my father. Even if their houses weren't empirically beautiful with classic, traditional architecture anchored by art from David Hockney, Kenneth Noland, and William Merritt Chase, their taste would have to be among those I most admire because those interiors were so intrinsically connected to the Burdens, my favorite people. However, the houses *were* empirically beautiful, so those rooms and the influences they embodied have seeped into my soul.

> "...you can love grandeur and amazing things and want to be surrounded by great beauty but still be a totally normal person."

While the Burdens had a house in Water Mill that was the site of many of my best childhood moments, pound for pound, the apartment they had on New York's Fifth Avenue, with its handsome woodwork and ingenious architraves, wins out as having my favorite interiors of all time. From the drawing room, with its seemingly endless seating zones, to the library, a veritable feast for the eyes, each room somehow managed to be cozy and grand at the same time. What you understand of rooms when you are in your twenties versus what you understand as an adult decorator, are, of course, very different things. Once I was grown, I read the references to Emilio Terry in the ebonized colonnettes in the side library and was inspired by the Cuban architect and designer's work for the British Embassy in Paris. Emilio Terry's style was referred to as *Louis XVII style*, which would have been the natural chronological evolution of French design had the Revolution not happened. In the living room, I could identify the deep and affectionate respect for architect and collector par excellence Sir John Soane (see pages 165 to 171 for my love letter to him), and I appreciate the passion behind the collections that were assembled patiently over years and years of dedication and persistence.

What I really know of these rooms, as well as the clear message that I have received from them, is that you can love grandeur and amazing things and want to be surrounded by great beauty but still be a totally normal person. It is up to the inhabitant to be comfortable and cozy and not up to the room. We don't have to choose. You can honor both impulses to live quotidian lives surrounded by visual magnificence. So, in that regard, the Burdens modeled for me how I want to live.

OPPOSITE: The entryway to the Burdens' Fifth Avenue apartment opens with a bang of chic exuberance pairing the Egyptian table, supported by pharaoh atlantes, and *Hotel L'Arbois, Sainte Maxime* painted by pop art iconoclast David Hockney.

The Egyptian-themed artifacts extend from the entryway into the living room. With ceilings this high, why wouldn't you put a statue above the entryway with such rich architrave, frieze, and cornice treatments.

To design a living room that can be simultaneously cozy and grand seems an impossible task
yet here it is. The multiple zones of seating invite people to get comfortable with a book from
the mahogany bookcases, which amplify the height of the ceilings and create another plane
from which to hang fabulous drawings.

OPPOSITE: The variety of display options abound in this room. Some collections are set at a low register on a human level; others are featured high on the colossally proportioned bookshelf. Regardless of the position, they are scattered about, not preciously displayed in a void of worship.

LEFT, TOP: The intimacy of this room is unique in an apartment of large spaces, but the message is the same: It's important to live with beautiful objects and cherished treasures in our daily lives. Here, a Spanish trunk serves as a telephone table. The room is enveloped in Clarence House's "Arts and Crafts" linen.

LEFT, CENTER: Chintz walls, a William Kent console, Georgian mantel, and William IV table surrounded by Regency chairs pull together this dining room.

LEFT, BOTTOM: I do some of my best work while soaking in the bathtub, so I have always appreciated Carter's decision to create a bathroom/boudoir office full of neoclassical elements that looks like the perfect refuge to me. (The toilet is hidden behind the Gothic screen.)

From the thin columns along the bookshelves and Egyptian bibelots on the mantel to the fireplace surround and coffee table, the Burdens' side library contains some of my favorite examples of how potently black can be used to punctuate exceptional decor.

ANTIQUARIAN NIALL SMITH

Of all the people who speak the language of design—be they artists, architects, fashion designers, interior decorators, and anyone concerned with domestic beauty writ large, from highbrow to lowbrow and anywhere in between—a distinct few possess the rare quality of having a fluency that is pitch-perfect, and their rooms and collections broadcast that mastery. Examples of these unicorns are people such as Madeleine Castaing, John Richardson, Elsie de Wolfe, or the Duke and Duchess of Windsor. These figures are not simply stylish people; they are obviously brilliant, educated, and cultured. And creating a beautiful life is their art form.

For me, an example of such a living, breathing Nobel Prize laureate in the language of design is Niall Smith, an Irish-born antiquarian who was generous enough to have shared his flawless taste with a generation (or two or three) of designers and civilians alike at his wonderful shop, Niall Smith Antiques, an ur-classical oasis. Like his offerings, the clients who came through the door were no ordinary beings—Paloma Picasso, Bill Blass—and they, too, had a mastery of the language as poet laureates.

During my career, I spent much time shopping at Niall's as it bebopped around New York City, and each time I was transported to another era. In every location, Niall not only showed his bonny wares but he also adapted them from storefront to loft to boutique—and that may very well have been part of his gift: fitting in flawlessly wherever he landed. Although his shop may be gone, Niall's legendary taste lives on in the pieces of history he procured and that many of us, his decorating clients, got to place with happy homeowners.

> "Then, just as now, grand tour souvenirs, marble busts, and finely made furniture beguiled me."

LEFT: Niall's living room is the epitome of low-key grandeur bedecked with Biedermeier chairs, a tufted chesterfield sofa, and laurel-leaf decorated bookshelves.

ABOVE: Neoclassical furniture, like beautifully made wood furniture, pairs well with everything. It's like the Riesling of decorating styles. (Though it won't surprise you to know that I love a gutsy Bordeaux too.)

LEFT: An ingenious way to display books when the shelves are showcasing things that can't sit on the floor.

OPPOSITE: There is not a single object in Niall's home that I wouldn't love to have in my own home.

ABOVE: Niall's collection of Biedermeier furniture, especially the Viennese-made table and chairs, exemplify why this style of furniture made during the early to mid-nineteenth century remains popular today.

OPPOSITE, TOP: An iron table surrounded metal French Nouveau chairs in Niall's New York loft apartment. This room could just as easily be in Rome or Paris. Its classical beauty defies its geographic setting.

OPPOSITE, BOTTOM: I'm pretty sure Niall's grand-tour collection is to blame for my own lifelong obsession. From Roman ruins to tazzas to sarcophagi, Niall's collection is unbeatable.

CHAPTER 2

PIVOTING
TO 7G

AS LUCK WOULD HAVE IT, my boy-friend, Pavlos, and I didn't have to move very far after Gaby got married and left 12C. It was 1997, and I was twenty-six. He finally got rid of his apartment (which we will henceforth call Alexa's closet number-two), and we were determined to get a real place that was ours. Shacking up officially with a new boyfriend might have seemed a big gamble had my instincts not yielded a full house and a winning hand. He is still very much my king of hearts.

Pavlos and I were entirely committed to living in sin (and in style) and we didn't need a second bedroom, so we swapped apartments with another couple in the building who were renting a one-bedroom off the other elevator bank. Although the new apartment was in the back of the building and on a lower floor, we were elated in that Baz Luhrmann *Romeo + Juliet* kind of way—just without the poison, swords, and imminent death.

Apartment 7G was not even six hundred square feet, and it lacked 12C's high ceilings, fireplace, entry hall, and a full two-thirds of its kitchen, so the space was smaller in every conceivable dimension. The need to pare down any unnecessary belongings was essential before any decorating could commence (though that didn't really stop me). As George Carlin has told us, "Life is really just trying to find a place for one's stuff, so you can go out and get more stuff." And, as he famously asked, "Have you ever noticed how your shit is stuff and everyone else's stuff is shit?" Well, funny he should ask because I have noticed and I believe it to be entirely true.

OPPOSITE: In my mid-twenties I had the budget to either buy artwork or have it framed; I could not afford both. Thankfully, I could paint. The lion is a watercolor I did of said animal at the entry of San Simeon. The oil painting is one I painted from a photo of an empty vestibule at Boughton House. I painted the amaryllis in high school, and it now resides with a friend in a house we designed together in Pass Christian, Mississippi, for her family. Finally, there hangs above an end table a small frieze of a beloved lion. (Happily, its fellow friezes have gotten larger and more numerous as I've aged.)

THE PERFECT MIX OF DARK AND COOL

The first decision that I made was to paint the apartment a rich dark brown. My father taught me (and anyone else who has read his amazing book *Mark Hampton On Decorating*) that painting small rooms a dark color will make them appear larger than they are because the edges disappear in the shadows of their corners, making the perimeter of the room harder to define. Naturally, my father's sage advice and decorating sensibilities were reflected in my design choices for this apartment because my own distinct tastes and passions were still percolating, not yet fully formed by the crucible of life.

Choosing to paint both the living room and the bedroom (the only rooms in the apartment) the same color would lend a sense of coherence to the somewhat eclectic mingling of belongings common to most twenty-somethings. I also know this to be true because I started by painting the bedroom an aqua blue, and it just didn't work. In any case, Benjamin Moore's Middlebury Brown (HC-68) was the perfect mix of dark and cool to enhance the illusion of spaciousness and provide a strong backbone for the rest of the design. Besides, one of my favorite rooms when I was growing up, as you now know, was our living room in Southampton. It, too, was a chocolate brown, though it is more Benjamin Moore

HC-67 than HC-68. It has additional red in it and is hotter. Mine felt crisper and it is a forever favorite.

Monochromatic schemes carry a lot of design weight. So, what I lacked in square footage, I would make up for in design strategy. Decorating legends Syrie Maugham and Albert Hadley were masters of monochromatic palettes, and their rooms showed how powerfully dramatic restraint can be. And while my color choice was restrained, my appetite for collecting objects that I find beautiful could not be described as such—not then, not now.

OPPOSITE: My homemade artwork outstayed its welcome by necessity. This is my pastel copy of Manet's painting of his friend and contemporary Berthe Morisot. Manet is one of my favorite painters.

OVERLEAF: When I was in my late teens or early twenties, I bought a beautiful Aptware tazza, which my father also thought was striking. He was running late and needed a birthday present for Bill Blass, so he took it. I was furious, but his response was, "Let's be clear, you obviously bought that on my dime, and I need a present, so I'm taking it." These gorgeous Aptware urns were thus paid for with my salary—so no one was taking them. I bought them from A. Smith, Billy Baldwin's late colleague whose office I now call my own.

TAPROOTS
RUN DEEP

Traditional design elements seemed to be a natural choice given my father's influence, where I was in life, and how I wanted to live. Tradition in design can be expressed in many ways and used as an anchor to provide a stabilizing mooring. The Roman busts, obelisks, and Aptware urns of my early collecting provided me a lodestar with which to explore different styles without getting too lost down any wayward paths. As many young adult children of traditionalists do, I assumed that the taste connected to my understanding of my parents' house is akin to declaring that I, too, am an adult. Also, collecting and amassing things felt like it suggested my having a point of view. I'm not sure that viewpoint was an entirely articulate one, but it was beginning to take some shape.

Two Regency bookshelves that my father designed for Hickory Chair lent architectural interest to the space where such details were lacking. The books themselves were arranged to take on structural importance while still being useful and accessible. The dark brown walls provided the perfect foil to emphasize the colors of the book jackets on the shelves, and I always fondly think of Billy Baldwin's work in Cole Porter's Waldorf apartments as a guide for the ultimate books-as-walls interior.

Our De Angelis sofa, grabbed from my father's storage and re-covered in a Clarence House Velour Cauchois, was another item with which I couldn't bear to part, and rightfully so because it was a key component to ensure that we could really kick back and watch my video cassettes of the complete *Highlander* series (sadly, I am not kidding) on the 14-inch TV/VCR combo (see right foreground in the photo). The zebra rug was my declaration of love for Albert Hadley. Another of my most prized possessions from that apartment is the first piece of custom upholstery that I ever commissioned for myself—with funds procured by selling my first car, a black Volkswagen Jetta (complete with its black fuzzy dice)—a Bridgewater chair made by Guido De Angelis, the hallowed New York upholsterer. At the time, Pavlos asked me how I could consider selling a car for a chair. I told him point-blank, "You're either in or you're out. From here it is only going to get worse." (Indeed, it did and it continues to, still.)

NO ROOM IS COMPLETE
WITHOUT BOOKS

Dark walls and a slew of upright book spines in bookcases also provide a repetitive, graphic illusion of order, which help to mitigate the tendency I have to teeter on the edge of (or dive right into) clutter. Although I cleared out so much stuff before the move, certain things—books, my father's paintings, grand tour souvenirs—simply could not be spared. Even as a budding bibliophile (I wish), the thought of giving up my books was a nonstarter. When I say no room is complete without books, I really mean it.

Living with a lot of books in a rental apartment, however, poses some design challenges, especially when one is young. To make permanent changes to an impermanent space would have been foolish. I hadn't fully appreciated how skillfully my parents had corralled all the books we had at home until it was time for me to face this challenge. Growing up in their house, we had books in every room, so it only made sense that I would want to re-create that same level of comfort that being surrounded by books provided me, only on my own. Books are the soul of humanity and to live without them is tantamount to living in a mausoleum, methinks.

Making my refuge with Pavlos would be anything but lifeless. I wanted it to be warm, inviting, and comfortable, evocative of what I imagined my parents' own earlier apartments were like as a young couple living in New York in the 1970s, only less disco. Having received many of my father's birthday-card paintings and hanging other figurative pieces of my own gave the apartment an air of sophistication likely well beyond my years.

RIGHT: Like my father, I like to draw and paint (though now it's a bit like pulling teeth). Dedicating a corner of this apartment to my easel and paints in that very small space shows how much I was trying to be productive (and how stalwart Pavlos was in ceding me the space it often required). One of my father's drawings of a nude hangs above a bookshelf he designed for his Hickory Chair collection, surrounded by watercolors of his and drawings of mine. The slipper chairs, also made by De Angelis, mimicked those in the Christie's sale of Givenchy's furniture that so captivated all of us decorators in the early 1990s.

Clearly dark brown has been in my decorating canon since I was in utero and is something I hope to never outgrow. The bedside tables were a model that I adapted for myself, and later entered into my furniture line because they were just too darned good not to share. The coromandel screen belonged to my Aunt Paula and reminds me of the one that still stands in my parents' Park Avenue apartment.

SHELTER FROM THE STORM

Furniture pieces along with the treasured paintings and objects inspired by my parents would be necessary comforts because this was the apartment that provided shelter and structure for me when I faced the untimely passing of my dear father in the summer of 1998. He died on July 23,* and it bizarrely hailed that day in New York—proof to me that the universe was as heartbroken as I. Pavlos didn't want me associating my grief with our apartment, so he rented us a hotel room for a few nights. Only afterward did we reflect upon his choice of hotel: The Mark. Naturally, I stole an umbrella.

Earlier that year, Marian McEvoy (who along with Paige Rense has served as a fairy godmother to me, whether realizing it or not) had asked me if she could publish pictures of this apartment in *Elle Decor*. Knowing the importance of having one's houses photographed and published (and in such an esteemed magazine, no less), I was beyond thrilled. The plan was to have my father write the article. I so wish he could have! I'd love to read his take on the influences present and accounted for in Pavlos's and my little den of iniquity. He wouldn't have failed to register the obvious Hadley–Hampton references. But I'm sure he would have had fascinating takeaways and insights beyond that.

He was a born scholar, and everything that filtered through his decorating data bank of a brain tied into the fields of art, history, architecture, and design. Much has been said about my father's incredible memory, but it is worth mentioning again. He always had his facts at the ready. When I was seventeen and reading a biography of Catherine the Great, I remember ambling down the stairs in Southampton and breezily asking him if he knew she'd been a German princess. His reply, "Of course. She was Princess von Anhalt-Zerbst of Stettin." He was like an endless party trick this way, which, sadly, encouraged the consequential atrophy of my mother's and my memory in turn. When he died, we realized with horror that we might never recall a person's name again.

Pardon me, but I must also add a little gallows humor here and share two of my favorite off-color stories about my father's death. One day, my father came home with a few big shopping bags. I was at their apartment—why, I don't know, but I was—and he essentially walked right into me. He had a weird, half-sheepish/half-sour look on his face, and I asked him why. He told me, "Well, I'm so skinny

from the chemo, none of my Anderson & Sheppard suits fit. But, today, I was walking by Armani and they were having a two-for-one sale; so, I got some new suits."

"Why is that making you frown?" I asked.

"Well," he said "as you know, I'm superstitious. I feel like now that I have bought these, I'm going to die."

"Don't worry," I said, "we'll bury you in one of them."

"Oh my God, eternity in Armani—NEVER! Promise you'll have me buried in one of my Anderson & Sheppard suits!" he exhorted.

"Done!" I answered. We cracked up in laughter. I know it's creepy, but sometimes you take humor where you can find it.

For the record, my father, a Hall of Fame member of the International Best Dressed List, was lovingly laid to rest in one of his bespoke English pin-striped suits, dark tie, pocket square, and his favorite John Lobb shoes. He lies near a leafy tree, under the shade cast by a beautiful obelisk (the design of which was taken from one that he placed in our Southampton garden) in the nondenominational Oakland Cemetery in Sag Harbor, close to dear friends and several artists, including Balanchine, whom he much admired.

Here's the second dark joke and I'll stop, I swear. Okay, so let me set the stage. It was the day his obituary came out in the *New York Times*. We had the great good fortune that Mitchell Owens, our respected friend, was its author. At the time, my sister was twenty-nine and I was twenty-seven. Among the information given, it said Mark and Duane were married for twenty-three years. They had actually been married for thirty-four. Instead of decrying the mistake, my mother turned to my sister and me, a sanguine look affixed to her face, and said, "I'm so sorry you girls had to find out this way." Again, hilarity ensued. We are an odd bunch, which no one shall deny.

---

*My daughter was born on this very day, ten years after his death, rehabilitating the date as a happy day, forever after.

OPPOSITE: Here, a Lee Jofa linen print, *Hydrangea Bird*, comprises the headboard and dust ruffle, which I combined with a custom-colored linen embroidery from Dek Tillett and antique needlepoint pillows. The drawing in the center is of my father by Henry Koehler.

A BRIDE'S SEND-OFF

Pavlos and I rented 7G until the whole building converted into co-op apartments and we had the opportunity to buy a unit on the tenth floor (technically speaking, we bought shares in the corporation that owned the building, which then leased us the desired apartment). Because we were already renters, we were considered "sponsored" tenants able to be fast-tracked to join the co-op. As anyone who has lived in New York is aware, it can be very difficult to be approved by co-op boards, especially when one is young. Being able to buy that first apartment was an incredible advantage for which we will forever be so grateful!

Unit 7G was also our home when Pavlos and I got married. The Saturday before our wedding in Greece, while I was packing my bags, I pulled out a Cover Girl blush, bought for the occasion. I was just taking off the wrapping with my teeth, as women do the world over, and poof, out went half of my front tooth! You can imagine my hysteria. We were due at the airport within a few hours. How was I going to cop to this to Pavlos and my mother? They were going to kill me! Pavlos came home and saw the alarm plastered on my closed-mouth mug. I placed my hand to block the lower half of my face to better confess what I had done and what had resulted. He very gently told me to show him. I moved my hand and smiled at him, showing the damage. His eyes started to twinkle, and he said, "It's amazing how such a small thing can have such a huge effect." I threw the blush at his head as he started laughing.

Somehow I found an emergency cosmetic dentist to fix my tooth, and I rushed to get to the airport. As I walked up to my mother and betrothed while they waited for me at the Delta terminal, they both grinned at me in greeting. They had each affixed a piece of black tape to one of their front teeth. I was unamused.

When Pavlos and I came back from our wedding, it would be a few months before we moved into the new apartment at 10E. I couldn't face unpacking after our three-week honeymoon-a-palooza that saw us tackle Paris, the Loire Valley, Venice, Florence, Rome, and a final victory lap to Athens before our ultimate return home.

I am a procrastinator by nature and the apartment was small. I couldn't figure out how I was going to get the clothes out and sorted in any proper order without dying under the ensuing avalanche. The dry-cleaning bill was also looming large and paralyzing me. Some time passed. Some more time passed. Eventually, I had to face it and apologize to Pavlos, promising to tackle it. "Don't worry," he said, "I was upset a few weeks ago. Now I realize that this is just a time capsule so that people in the future will learn what women wore in the year 2000." Finally, I unpacked.

ABOVE: New Yorkers are known for our resourcefulness when it comes to making due when space is in short supply. The bed was called into duty as a desk during the daytime.

OPPOSITE: I will always love the rich variety of colors in natural stone, from the suppleness of white marble in the bust to the delicate veins in the obelisks.

The original version of David Hicks's Etruscan red bedroom with its grand canopy bed situated in the middle of the room has redefined bedroom decor for me for all time.

DAVID HICKS

As some design followers reading these love notes might already know, my father's first design job was working for the most sought-after decorator of the swinging 1960s—David Hicks. This English decorator is famous for his iconic use of bold colors, geometrically patterned carpets, and masterful blending of pedigreed antiques with modern lines. Mark was just a student in the spring semester of his undergraduate junior year abroad in London when he worked for David. My father always worked during the summers, of course (once he even chauffeured Jayne Mansfield when she appeared in Indianapolis), but this was his first design job. Years later, when he moved to New York with my mother, he even became David's New York associate before ultimately joining McMillen, Inc. So, while David Hicks's influence will eternally reverberate throughout the design world with great force, I'd like to think that his place of honor in the Hampton family is even more firmly entrenched. In fact, I almost don't know where to begin.

I will start by mentioning that our New York apartment in the early 1970s was full of David Hicks's carpets, fabrics, and colors. The first decorated rooms that I ever saw—meaning those in our Park Avenue home—were rife with meaningful doses of Hicksian DNA. Naturally, at the time, I could not identify them as such, but I loved noting them later when they became obvious to my decorating self. My father was clearly my mentor, and David was his. So, I like to think of David as my mentor once removed, and I am grateful for whatever exposure I have had to that extraordinarily talented man, even if in reality there is a design generation separating us.*

The first time that I remember being with the Hicks family was as a child when we were visiting them in the English countryside. It was then that I first met his incredible son Ashley and his amazing daughter India, both of whom I now adore and admire. I recall the house, David's library, with its wall upholstery made of his mother's velvet dress, the red book spines popping off the dark walls, and the glow of the lighting—it was so dramatic and lush that I can still feel my wonder. The living room was crisp and fresh, with an exciting color

> "I could happily live in either version forever and never become disenchanted."

palette and bold carpet, though it was simultaneously traditional with Louis XVI chairs, a gilded Directoire mantel clock, and Chinese ginger jars. Large-scale portraits conferred grandeur and history upon its interior, working to create a room that was very much what I'm sure I assumed it should be for a man such as Mr. Hicks and his wife, Lady Pamela, daughter of Lord Mountbatten. I look at pictures of those rooms now and know that if they had been designed yesterday, their beauty would be met with as much fanfare and praise as they surely must have been when first conceived and delivered hot off the presses.

However, of all the places in which David Hicks lived and decorated, my absolute favorite, hands down, was his set of rooms in Albany. While I never set foot in Albany—neither New York's state capital nor the residential building in London—I know its iterations as well as I know any rooms in which I've lived. Whether it's the rich Etruscan red version with its amazing silk-damask canopy bed or the re-envisioned brown version with its adjacent butter-yellow entry hall hung with plasters, I could happily live in either version forever and never become disenchanted. (Although if forced at gunpoint to choose, I'd likely go with the original red rooms. The red incarnation was inspired by the rooms of the 1830s, and as renowned design editor Stephen Drucker once articulated for me over dinner together, when I mentioned loving the 1840s, "Yes, you have an obvious love of the nineteenth century." Who knew? I guess knowing yourself truly is one of the most difficult things in life.)

Working at Mark Hampton meant hearing, repeatedly, that purple was verboten (his allowance of pale lavender notwithstanding). It troubled me for some time when I started to realize as an adult that I couldn't help but be drawn to that favorite color of my childhood. At the age of twelve, I used to prance around in purple

---

*My father would occasionally drop gems like this one. "You know when David Hicks told me to use moiré?" he asked me. "No, Daddy, when?" I replied. "Never!" came the response. It still cracks me up.

In its original Etruscan red version, it boasts furniture (including the gilded swan chairs) inherited from Hicks's mother-in-law, Countess Edwina Mountbatten. To die for.

The mid-1990s version of David's set of rooms in Albany with its dramatic walls and astonishing George II tables with gilded eagles is a first impression one is unlikely to forget.

Gloria Vanderbilt jeans and a purple-and-white-striped shirt, bedecking it all with a purple felt hat. Retrospectively, this may, in fact, be the very genesis of my father's falling out with that color. In any case, now I cannot imagine decorating without purple, and I attribute it all to the long-gestating influence of David Hicks's brilliant and jarring color palette. I know in my bones that if my father were beamed back into existence and faced with my current purple bedroom, he would find it fabulous—because it is.

ABOVE: The star of unorthodox and inventive color combinations in the English countryside library is the dark-red velvet surrounding the fireplace made from one of his mother's dresses.

OPPOSITE: The living room in the Oxford house is at once pedigreed and refreshingly modern with a lively color scheme and mix of Louis XVI, neoclassical, and regency pieces. Studying signature David Hicks's color combinations has emboldened me as I've grown in age and power. Certainly, he is the master but he teaches us all that we needn't be tepid to be chic.

BILL BLASS

The interiors of acclaimed fashion designers have long held me in their thrall. Oscar de la Renta: check. Yves Saint Laurent: check. Valentino: check. I find their houses profound because they show those individuals flexing muscles we seldom see them use in their public lives. Within the confines of their profession, their tastes have to shake, rattle, and roll. They need to endlessly and enthusiastically innovate—at least two times a year, and nowadays even more—in ways totally unique, but, also, always in step with what I would call their greater sensibility, or what everyone else would now call "their brand." (If ever there were a grimmer, less inspirational term, someone be sure to tell me, please.)

When fashion designers get to design for themselves, they wrestle with permanence. They are not momentarily going to be swapping out all the textiles. They are not being inspired by their muse or their house model. In their domiciles, they don't need to consider gender or fashion or even the economy, for the most part. Nothing is ephemeral. What a wonderful freedom they must feel, and how strange and heady it must seem when they really let loose and go for it.

Bill Blass went for it. But when I say he went for it, I certainly don't mean red-and-white polka-dot curtains, or gold dripping off of every surface. His taste very much correlated to his unstuffy, effortlessly manicured designs for dresses and suits. Bill's style was all gutsy restraint and unerring good taste. This has to be where I was first infected with my love of helmets and military trophies. Perhaps this obsession was topped off by visits to the State Hermitage Museum in Leningrad in 1988 during perestroika, and again years ago to open Design Week in Saint Petersburg. However, I first noticed such things in an actual apartment being lived among by Bill, himself a veteran of World War II.

When I was younger, Bill lived right next door to my dermatologist. The hideousness of those appointments was softened by their proximity to the altar of my hero worship. I thought his apartment on East Fifty-Seventh Street was beyond magical. Then Bill did the unthinkable—he left it. When I first heard of his moving, I was filled with sadness and dread. I hated to think that the apartment

> "Bill's style was all gutsy restraint and unerring good taste."

that I loved so much for so long was going to disappear. Well, the king is dead, long live the king!

While at his old address, he had been living in what I would describe as a "normal" apartment, grand but befitting a single occupant. What Bill created in his new place, with the assistance of his dear friends Chessy Rayner and Mica Ertegun of MAC II, was something else entirely. This was not a normal apartment at all, but an installation of precise beauty and a display of object erudition. (The Burdens, see page 41, win for regular erudition with their vast quantities of first-edition books, all of which I am sure were read.) Bill's space had a sense of reverence about it and displayed his authentic and genius personal style.

Even better was that, again, here was someone for whom I cared deeply, perhaps even venerated, living in the space. Bill had long been lending me beautiful dresses to wear as a teen, when I was skinny in addition to being tall. I could come to his atelier and look through the racks, just making sure to return the dress (and sometimes shoes too!) later in the week. Bill made my graduation dress, and later, I walked down the aisle in a Bill Blass dress that was a version of a scarlet dress he had made for my mother (with my bridesmaids wearing amazingly beautiful Oscar de la Rentas). So, Bill was both an idol and a sweet and generous family friend.

Seeing the beauty of his rooms only cemented his status in my imagination as the great man he was. Bill's apartment and his house in the country were exercises in perfection and precision. Although they were definitely decorated and decorative, the interiors were also boiled down. The objects within had a graphic quality that made sense both in their relationship to one another and alone in the space he gave them. And, somehow, while there was nothing humble about the room's designs, there was a real dignity about his interiors.

OPPOSITE: Bill Blass, like my father, hailed from Indiana, and both make up two of my biggest design heroes. The entryway to Bill's apartment feels to me like I am stepping into an axonometric Piranesi drawing of space.

Interestingly, in his New York apartment, his bed was in the corner of the immense room that also served as part sitting room, part library. I remember thinking how unexpected a choice this was. Most of us, after all, would have placed our beds dead center, as though encouraging the enactment of a regal, daily levée. But not Bill. His presence in the room was a secondary focus to the impact of everything else. That was so him.

Bill famously loved Hollywood, and his interiors were, for the most part, white and brown, suggestive of black-and-white movies (notably, his bed was a rich red paisley). He loved Clark Gable above all and if you look at Bill's own publicity shots, you can see similarities between them—both were so handsome with such twinkling eyes.

My favorite story to share about Bill is one in which he was telling me a tale of his personally espying film stars once when he was in Rome. He said he spotted Ava Gardner in flagrante in the early hours one morning, making love to a man on the banks of the Tiber. After telling me the story and regaling me with the outrageousness of it all, I asked him, "Bill, why don't you tell me what *you* were doing by the river at dawn?" Without missing a beat, he replied, "Swimming against the current, as always."

Upon Bill's death came the immense Sotheby's sale that captured the interest of the world over. Walking through the lots, I found a pencil drawing of mine that I had given to him one year for his birthday, a copy of Delacroix's own self-portrait. It was labeled "Drawing by an unknown twentieth-century artist." My mother and I had a good laugh, agreeing that the attribution could not be more dead-on in its accuracy.

That Sotheby's sale transformed the world of design for those who had not been lucky enough to see all of its contents in situ, in person. It remains one of the very best sales that ever was.

ABOVE: Everything in Bill's home was of exquisite quality, and this was evident to all who witnessed and bid on his belongings. The pair of ormolu and bronze bear sconces on his walls were estimated to sell for twenty-two thousand dollars, but ultimately, after fierce bidding, typical throughout the entire three-day auction, sold for more than three hundred thousand.

OPPOSITE: Bill was an avid collector with an impeccable eye, and the 2003 Sotheby's auction of Bill's estate is a testament to that. The auction generated $13.6 million (twice as much as estimated) for two charities: AIDS Care Center at New York Presbyterian Hospital and the Metropolitan Museum of Art. His philanthropy was on par with his design legacy.

Bill loved all things Hollywood and had a penchant for Regency, but not necessarily Hollywood Regency. Amid the sobriety of his Sutton Place apartment sits the carved lion's head and feet on this pair of Regency daybeds, circa 1810, showing how quietly good design can roar without being flashy.

CLOCKWISE FROM TOP LEFT: Bill loved collecting military memorabilia. A bronze statue of Napoleon Bonaparte on horseback anchored the window wall of Bill's bedroom with his red-and-orange-paisley bed tucked aside discretely in a corner.

The ebonized spoon-back klismos was just one of the many beautiful Regency pieces that Bill used to furnish his apartment in the city and house in the country (pictured here). And the artwork! Everything Bill touched was chic. Serenity and sophistication are hallmarks of his style.

If David Hicks's red canopied bed in the middle of the room is on one side of the bed-placement spectrum, then Bill Blass would sit on the opposite end (literally and figuratively).

CHAPTER 3

BUYING OUR
FIRST HOME, 10E

AFTER OUR BIG FAT Greek wedding in Pavlos's homeland in 2000, we settled into our new place as proud homeowners of 10E, a two-bedroom apartment with a fireplace. We were moving on up in the world, literally by three floors! This apartment was situated toward the front of the building, so expansive Manhattan vistas and abundant sunshine greeted us daily. These gorgeous views helped us overlook the ridiculous glass fuses in the fuse box, arched uncased doorways from which Tom and Jerry might emerge, a kitchen so old that I wouldn't want to make coffee—much less cook—in it, and other dated foibles. It's amazing how the magic of sunshine can ease otherwise unbearable features. Besides, this apartment wasn't a rental; it was all ours, and we could alter it to fit our needs and aesthetic proclivities.

Rounding out my twenties at the start of a new century and living in a new apartment with my beloved as homeowners filled me with hope and optimism. The nonsense about Y2K and the potential collapse of modern society didn't faze me one bit. In 2000, I also ventured into a new enterprise, establishing Alexa Hampton, Inc., which was dedicated to the nascent product lines that I hoped to have while continuing to lead my father's firm.

Everything was happening! What wasn't happening was the use of bold colors in this apartment, for which I had my reasons.

As a young couple, Pavlos and I knew we were incredibly lucky to have gotten through the co-op board gauntlet to be able to buy the apartment, but we weren't sure exactly how long we'd be staying. This hesitancy revealed itself in the design choices and the updates we made, or precisely, *didn't* make initially. Investing in big-ticket items such as an upgraded electrical system and kitchen was necessary, so though I daydreamed nonstop about this apartment and envisioned every last detail, we played it safe with color, and I stuck to what I knew would appeal to us as well as a potential new buyer, should we need to find one. I was also under sway of Bill Blass's color palette of ivory, whites, and browns. In adopting them here, I felt like I was lending seriousness to the endeavor.

OPPOSITE: The magic in the living room came from the beautiful antique marble mantel (which I purchased at Asta and have since reproduced for my line with Chesney's) alongside a big black Napoleon III bookcase.

I left the windows undressed to maximize the view of the city outside, while extra-tall mirrored folding screens work to reflect the light deeper into the room.

BRASS TACKS

The benefit of buying a co-op that had previously been a rental is that we didn't have to contend with decades of bad renovations from a hodgepodge of various owners that would all need to be undone. On the flip side, that meant there was considerable construction with which to contend. I detail much of that makeover in my first book, *The Language of Interior Design*, but for your benefit, dear reader, I'll provide a short list here: We overhauled the electrical, all lighting, and the HVAC systems; gutted the kitchen; added molding (both crown and base); ebonized the floors; and redesigned the passageways with paneled mahogany doors that I devised. Bathrooms seemed too much of a commitment if we were to move in three years, so why bother?

My new homeowner's trepidation also meant no unnecessary curtains. As I was doing this apartment, I was simultaneously installing interiors in a fifteen-thousand-square-foot, four-bedroom house of great distinction in the South. The curtains for that home were extraordinary, made with exacting love by our long-time collaborator Anthony Lawrence-Belfair. And they cost a small (perhaps even medium) fortune. When my clients saw me publicly embracing no curtains in a newspaper article, they sat up and took notice. The husband of the married duo tore out the page, circled my quotation decrying the need for curtains, and wrote in the margins, "That's great. Cancel my order!" He was very cheeky, and I learned never to champion anything as ridiculous as a house not needing curtains ever again.

Back to our apartment. The living room's furniture plan came together almost instantaneously because of the fixed placement of the fireplace and the windows. To avoid having our backs face the casement windows and to respect the axis point of the fireplace required situating the sofa along the west wall. Both my husband and I are tall, so an extra-deep, very long sofa would ensure we could both lounge comfortably. Along with my beloved De Angelis Bridgewater chair and dark brown slipper chairs à la the ones in Givenchy's 1993 Christie's auction, I "liberated" a pair of antique bergère frames that

were left forgotten in the firm's storage space. I covered the bergères in canvas to make them a little less formal—just like me.

While I don't practice a lot of formality and structure in much of my personal life, there is no tempering my love of classical design and architectural elements when it comes to decorating my own house. With the sofa along the west wall, opposing it were an antique Charles X marble fireplace with graceful volutes and a Louis XVI silvered mirror above the mantel. Throughout the apartment and especially in the living room, one couldn't help but notice my devotion to classical and neoclassical motifs as expressed by the artwork in the room (a painting I did of the Parthenon frieze hung above the sofa), numerous obelisks, miniature ruins, bas-relief profiles, Athenian and Spartan busts and helmets, along with more of my collection of grand tour mementos with which I am obsessed, as you know very well by now. Painting the walls a soft off-white and choosing a neutral color palette for the living room allowed these objets d'art (such as they were) to shine. Paying homage to the David Hicks rug that I had in my childhood bedroom, I designed the living room rug, which gave just the right touch of youthfulness—I was, after all, still in my twenties then.

OPPOSITE, CLOCKWISE FROM TOP: Campaign tables (table athenée) flanking the fireplace, given their designed portability, could easily be called to serve as drinks tables; and the slipper chairs easily moved.

One of the first tables I had built for me featured a classic motif, the Greek key. Atop it sits large marble spheres and another ancient gift from the earth, fossilized mud plates called septarian concretions, purchased at Cove Landing. On either side of my painting of a staircase from a Rothschild *hotels particulars* are two prints of Trajan's Column—a wedding present from the Pockers of the famous framing house.

My parents, and my Aunt Paula as well, always had specimen-marble samples at home, and as I grew older, I, too, became obsessed with collecting antique ones from the eighteenth and nineteenth centuries. I like arranging the smaller tablets en masse.

LIVING IN A GRECO-ROMAN BIVOUAC

It's no secret that I love many things Athenian and Greek, so much so that I married a Greek man. My upbringing, my parents, the places we traveled, and the books and movies I've consumed may have all contributed to this bending toward the ancients. Taste is so personal and idiosyncratic—who's to say where one's preferences originate? For me, the objects themselves are aesthetically pleasing because of their balanced symmetry, precision, and commendable craftsmanship. My love of grand tour souvenirs also extends to campaign furniture, which has been in use since Caesar's rule. Flanking the fireplace are Athenian campaign tables—just the slightest of nods to my love of campaign furniture of all types because of its portability and metamorphic qualities.

A feeling of wonderment overcomes me when my eye catches one of the campaign tables or helmets because, for a split second, I imagine myself living in a Greco-Roman bivouac with animal skins on the floor and warming myself next to a brazier (this may also be from those darn romance novels). While the traveling aspect appeals to me, the idea of living in a time when people cared so much about beauty in nearly every setting seems remarkable—and when the baseline aesthetic was of such high caliber that mounted soldiers' helmets had feathers on them. The fact that a hat was designed as such just bewitches me. From helmets and armor to candlesticks with little shields, maces, and axes carved on them, the objects in my home make me feel as if I'm living in a fairy tale, or at least remind me of one—you know the one where the Greek finds his lady love.

ABOVE: I painted the image of a Parthenon frieze that hangs above the sofa as a stand-in until I could afford something not made by me.

OPPOSITE: I sometimes enjoy arranging tablescapes according to color, such as this collection of onyx obelisks, sculpture, and patinaed metal chairs. Blue and black done well always makes me think of Madeleine Castaing.

ALWAYS A STUDENT

Originally, the second bedroom in 10E was slated to be a guest room, but with space at a premium, it made more sense to turn it into a study, which would get more use than a rarely occupied room. For its diminutive dimensions, I departed from the cool neutrals of the living room for richly textured toile de Jouy wall coverings featuring Egyptian icons such as sphinxes and obelisks.

The Billy Baldwin bookcase, itself iconic in the world of design, sat opposite an Irish Regency closed-up dining table that was bought from Cove Landing to serve as a desk. The mahogany table has an ebony inlaid apron carved with a Greek key design; it was a gift from my dear Greek husband. He dreamed of living in a home with a dining room—a rarity in New York City apartments. His dream would eventually come true, but until then the table served a valuable purpose as a writing table paired with the elegant curves of a klismos chair. With square footage in short supply, it was important to be flexible in our plans as a young couple and make efficient use of what we had. Klismos chairs and brass bookcases are, in my mind, natural components of any room.

ABOVE:: It feels like Sophie's Choice to have to choose a favorite chair, but if I must, it would be a klismos chair, with its ancient Greek origins.

OPPOSITE: Thankfully, I will never have to choose which books to cull from my library with ample shelving. For me, no room is complete without books. Books appear in every room of my home, not just the library, because they are a necessary and indispensable..

THE RENAISSANCE IN THE NORTH — THE METROPOLITAN MUSEUM OF ART

ITALIAN SPLENDOR
Great Palaces, Castles, and Villas

MODERN EUROPE — THE METROPOLITAN MUSEUM OF ART

THE RENAISSANCE IN ITALY AND SPAIN — THE METROPOLITAN MUSEUM OF ART

THE SPLENDOR OF FRANCE

LIVING IN STYLE PARIS

PALAZZI OF ROME

GREAT HOUSES OF ENGLAND & WALES
HUGH MONTGOMERY-MASSINGBERD   CHRISTOPHER SIMON SYKES

SINTRA · A LANDSCAPE WITH VILLAS   JOSE CORNELIO DA SILVA / GERALD LUCKHURST

Paintings from The Frick Collection   Frick/Abrams

BRERA   STORIA DELLA PINACOTECA E DELLE SUE COLLEZIONI   CANTINI

GEOFFREY BEENE · EARLY GEORGIAN · MID GEORGIAN · LATE GEORGIAN · SIENA THE GOTHIC DREAM · Swedish Style · LIVING WITH WHAT YOU LOVE · ARCHITECTURE OF THE ANCIENT CIVILIZATIONS IN COLOR · 18th CENTURY ENGLISH FURNITURE · THE DIANA COOPER SCRAPBOOK · BILLY BALDWIN decorates

Richard Ormond · SARGENT · John Singer Sargent Watercolors · A LIFE OF PICASSO JOHN RICHARDSON · A LIFE OF PICASSO JOHN RICHARDSON · A LIFE OF PICASSO JOHN RICHARDSON

THE YVES SAINT LAURENT PIERRE BERGÉ COLLECTION   CHRISTIE'S / Flammarion
THE SALE OF THE CENTURY

VENETIAN VILLAS: THE HISTORY AND CULTURE

The Great Libraries   From Antiquity to the Renaissance

ITALIAN PAINTING

KATE F. JENNINGS   JOHN SINGER SARGENT   Crescent Books

IMPRESSIONISM   BERNARD DENVIR
THE PAINTERS AND THE PAINTINGS

HENRI MATISSE   JAZZ   GEORGE BRAZILLER

AUTHENTIC DECOR · A History of American Art · EXTRAORDINARY FURNITURE Abrams

MARK HAMPTON An American Decorator   DUANE HAMPTON

FRANK LLOYD WRIGHT

FOR THE KING'S PLEASURE
THE FURNISHING & DECORATION OF GEORGE IV'S APARTMENTS AT WINDSOR CASTLE

Origins of
Impressionism   The Metropolitan Museum of Art

france-australia   a tradition of global enterprise   FOCUS

ANATOMY FOR THE ARTIST

DUBLIN · A GRAND TOUR
JACQUELINE O'BRIEN WITH DESMOND GUINNESS

FLOWERS   CAROLYNE ROEHM

ABOVE SYDNEY   George Hall

Turkey from the Air

IN THE PINK · DÉCOR · VOGUE & THE METROPOLITAN MUSEUM OF ART COSTUME INSTITUTE · GARDNER'S ART THROUGH THE AGES · MICHAEL FRIED MANET'S MODERNISM · STYLE AND SUBSTANCE · ENJOYING ROSES · ENGLISH Country · La natura morta in Italia

MASTER OF MY OWN DOMAIN

Decorating the principal bedroom in a home that we actually owned was particularly delightful. For our bedroom in 10E, I opted for a cool, icy blue palette, a departure from the rich dark brown of our bedroom in 7G. Expert colorist Pat Cutaneo helped me choose the wall color to pick up the hues of the Fortuny fabrics used in the upholstery in the bedroom. While Pavlos and I were in Venice during our honeymoon, I came across some gorgeous floral Fortuny fabric, which I just "had to have" for the headboard, dust ruffle, and chairs.

When we moved into this apartment, Pavlos and I were still new to homemaking as a married couple, so I played it safe with the color scheme. Blue-and-white rooms are a classic look that rarely, if ever, tires, and it served us well. White bedside tables corresponded to the crisp white crown molding and built-ins necessary to hide the heating and cooling units along the window wall. The radiator covers prevented me from having full curtain panels, so I opted for swags and jabots to dress the windows in arctic-blue taffeta trimmed in gold tape.

Gold touches were also in the frames of the watercolors, as well as in the light fixtures and door hardware. Swing-arm bedside lights allowed for adequate clearance while reading in bed, one of my favorite activities any time of day (when I could still read the font sizes of regular, nonlarge-print books). A nice contrast to the femininity of the room were the mahogany chest and the newly installed mahogany doors, which brought it all together.

ABOVE: Silver frames on the photos and gold frames around the watercolors along with the hardware in the headboard and chair were like jewelry to this bedroom.

OPPOSITE, TOP TO BOTTOM: My apartment building does not have particularly distinguished architecture such as one might see in a Parisian structure, for example, so traditional furniture works wonderfully with the framework that exists, and it's even better with the basic architectural elements that I added.

My blue-and-white bedroom was influenced by a watery-blue silk bedroom that my father designed for a client in Palm Beach.

EVOLUTIONS OVER TIME

Ultimately, Pavlos and I lived in 10E for six years, far longer than either of us could have imagined as newlyweds. During that span of time, so much in our lives and the world at large changed. Some events were hoped for and planned, such as expanding my product line to include fabrics with Kravet, furniture with Hickory Chair, carpets with STARK, and lighting designs with Visual Comfort. There was also my being named to the AD100 in 2002 for the first time, and the crowning jewel of my life's work: parenthood. Other events were completely unforeseeable (save for highly skilled astrologers or Nostradamus junkies).

The year after we moved into 10E, the Twin Towers fell during the terrorist attacks on September 11, 2001. Having grown up with the towers soaring past all the other skyscrapers, they were a point of reference that always directed me in the correct path when other landmarks were unfamiliar. I could always look around, spot the towers, and know which way was east or west with them in the southern tip of Manhattan. What happened that day was incomprehensible on so many levels.

At the time, Pavlos was working in the north tower of the World Financial Center. I was frantically trying to get ahold of him, but the cell phone towers had been destroyed along with the Twin Towers and nearly three thousand lives. As if in some sort of trance, I trudged up Park Avenue to my childhood apartment in an effort to piece together the news while I waited anxiously to hear from my husband. In all the confusion that ensued, only one thing was clear: Park Avenue was

no longer my home. Home was what Pavlos and I had built together.

By the miracle that is good luck, he and I reunited at the sturdy mahogany doors we chose together for 10E. We stayed ensconced in our apartment during the aftermath and confusion, which led many New Yorkers to decamp from the city. For me, that was inconceivable.

Two years later was the blackout of 2003, when every square inch of Manhattan as well as most of the Northeast from Provincetown, Massachusetts, to Lansing, Michigan, lost power. I had just completed a photo shoot for *Architectural Digest* and had to walk uptown in a miniskirt and stilettos to help the photographers leave the job site. Then, downtown I went. Barefoot, I plodded up ten flights of stairs to get home to Pavlos, who had pragmatically filled the bathtub so we could have water. My provisions were equally practical, consisting of a Heineken six-pack, Marlboro Lights, and two Charleston Chews. The look on Pavlos's face revealed his astonishment at my chosen priorities, but his displeasure faded as we watched the sun set, then had our Chews by candlelight.

OPPOSITE: When Pavlos and I chose mahogany doors for 10E, we knew only that we loved their stately quality. Never in a million years did we know then that we would eventually expand the footprint of 10E not just once but twice. Now when giving people a tour of our apartment, which I insist all innocent guests endure, I like to take them through all the "secret" hallways of my rabbit warren, a consequence of combining three separate apartments. Here, rows of plaster bas-reliefs guide people to one of three back doors, this one is next to our bar.

While not the actual bathroom where I was inspired to create my first line of the flush mounts for my friends at Visual Comfort, this is the current view from the tub where all my best ideas are now invented. And, as with elsewhere, even in my bathroom, there is some grand-tour appeal with porcupine-quill boxes (of which there were many scattered in the apartment), intaglios, and framed photos of helmets that adorn some historic Thomas Hope (1769–1821) furniture.

NECESSITY IS THE
MOTHER OF INVENTION

In 2006, while soaking in the bathtub and many months pregnant with twins, I was leaning back staring at the ceiling as one is wont to do when housing multiple people in their body. As a very recumbent person, I do some of my best problem-solving in the bathtub. Only this time, as I was looking at my ceiling, my gears were stuck wondering why I couldn't find a decent-looking flush-mounted light fixture. In fact, they all seemed fairly indecent, resembling droopy bosoms. Frustrated with my lack of options, I realized that I needed to create what I wanted. So I sent a letter to Andy Singer of Visual Comfort introducing myself and shortly afterward FedExed him five excellent designs for ceiling-mounted fixtures along with a binder of other drafts for lights that became the start of a successful partnership. I assume my tombstone will read: "Queen of the Flush Mount."

Later that fall, Pavlos and I welcomed the birth of our twin sons, Michalis and Markos. When I woke up that day, I instinctively knew the inhabitants of my gigantic belly who had been trying to kick their way out would have their release. I showered, made up my face (being sure to choose the very longest-wearing lipstick), packed a bag, and then called a fancy car service to take me to the hospital. Once there, I instructed the driver to head over to where I knew Pavlos was having lunch and called him to say, "I'm at the hospital. There is a car waiting for you outside. Come, let's meet our sons."

The study had been transformed to serve as the twin's nursery; needless to say, that wasn't the only thing in our apartment that changed. I did things that I never in a million years thought I would do to an interior. In our sunken living room that I had designed with such care, I removed all the furniture except for pieces at the very perimeter so that I could lay down interlocking padded-plastic floor tiles and put up an interior fence to pen in the boys. I needed to create a safe playspace (or what

> "While I don't practice a lot of formality and structure in much of my personal life, there is no tempering my love of classical design and architectural elements when it comes to decorating my own house."

looked like a jumbo baby jail) that blocked access to the stairs that lead to the adjacent hallway.

A year and a half after the twins were born, I was seven months pregnant with our daughter when my literary agent and dear friend William Clark approached me to say, "It's time." Previously, I held the belief that books by decorators were a catalogue raisonné, reserved for the end of one's career. While I am rarely at a loss for words, it had never occurred to me to become an author before an imminent retirement. But here I was, in my mid-thirties, leading my father's firm for eleven years without him and just brimming with ideas and projects. During both pregnancies, creative energy just flowed out of me. I had never paid much attention to chakras but there was no denying my sacral chakra was completely awakened.

Very shortly before our daughter, Aliki, affectionately known as Kiki, was born in 2008, we expanded our home by buying the one-bedroom apartment next door, 10D. It was a race to the finish as Pavlos and I both knew that once she entered the world, we would be very busy. We had just finished painting the very night before her arrival, and we were lying in our new bedroom drinking in the fumes from the oil paint. Pavlos turned to me and asked, "Is being in here while the paint dries okay for the baby?" "Yes," I said, "but we will be dead by morning." I am happy to say I was only joking. We lived and Kiki came without a hitch.

Those first few years of parenthood were extraordinarily magical and wild times. If I could do it all over again, I wouldn't change a thing, except possibly offering a proper chair (perhaps a favorite klismos or bergère) to visiting grandparents because beanbags proved to be particularly challenging for them to navigate. And once personal preference is stripped away, what is successful decorating at its core if not making sure that everyone who enters your home feels comfortable and welcomed?

MARK HAMPTON
WITH ANNE BASS

Anne Hendricks Bass, the late arts philanthropist with an erudite eye and an unparalleled art collection to show for it, had two vastly different residences in which to showcase her very personal collection of paintings, drawings, and sculptures. The architecture of her Fort Worth and New York apartments were at opposite ends of the spectrum—a Paul Rudolph modern manifesto in the West and a classic 1920s prewar aerie in the Northeast—and yet the through line of Anne's impeccable taste was felt everywhere. It's striking how her art collection appeared potently but differently in both of her residences.

My introduction to Anne Bass's world came when my father began working for the family in the 1980s. Our families became dear friends and, so, it was particularly fun to be allowed to see a different side of Anne and my father's friendship when they worked on her project at 960 Fifth Avenue. I was a young intern working at Mark Hampton when I installed Anne's bespoke leather-bound books in her beautiful library, teetering on a ladder in the high heels and mini-skirt that were my wardrobe staples at the time. Setting up anything in such gorgeous surroundings befitted my own interests and experience (or lack thereof).

The combined four years my father spent working with Anne on her apartment is a striking example of collaboration at its finest. Anne's art collection was germane to creating an interior with enduring beauty. Within the context of her traditional apartment, one's experience of the impressionist and abstract masterpieces it contained was electrified, creating a whole that was entirely more than the sum of its priceless parts; all combined, it was a gestalt reflection of the woman to whom the rooms belonged.

> "For my father, creating successful interiors meant understanding the owners' proclivities and presenting them thoughtfully as integral expressions of the design."

For my father, creating successful interiors meant understanding the owners' proclivities and presenting them thoughtfully as integral expressions of the design. From the moment you entered the apartment and were greeted by one of the world's most beloved and recognizable statues, Degas's *Petite danseuse de quatorze ans*, there was no mistaking where you were or what delighted the resident powerhouse patron and lifelong student of ballet.

Anne's devotion to the arts was multifaceted; she also loved architecture and gardening, which took their place in other rooms. The living room and dining room were perfect examples of how impactful juxtapositions can be when done masterfully. Pristine George II furniture in the living room's neutral color palette provided the perfect setting for the two Rothkos to do their powerful pas de deux. Yin and yang were further punctuated in the dining room, where moody Monets hung against mirrored panels bouncing light in every direction and off the metallic sheen on the legs of Mies van der Rohe dining chairs.

Canonical design references from a swath of eras in both rooms revealed the intellectual rigor present in the restrained craftsmanship and sophistication of the decor. Anne and Mark both had innate style, but in the creation of these interiors, their encyclopedic knowledge of global references and exacting standards were equally as important as a desire to create an elegantly stunning residence.

OPPOSITE: The opening salvo of Anne's apartment, with its sleek lacquered gray and cream walls and Degas's *Petite danseuse de quatorze ans* is a superlative example of an entryway's autobiographical declaration.

The juxtaposition between the angular lines of the high-contrast moldings and window panes create a harmony with the sweeping curves of the furniture and feminine appeal of Degas's *Femme en peignoir bleu le torse decouvert.*

ABOVE: In the living room, an immaculate set of curvaceous George II furniture covered in an icy neutral damask serves as the perfect foil to the big, bravura twin Rothkos.

OPPOSITE: The emotional punch from Rothko's bold paintings hits hard when in an atmosphere that is all restrained craftsmanship and sophistication apparent in Anne's living room.

ABOVE: The monochromatic colors chosen for the library expertly accentuate the gorgeous moldings throughout the room.

LEFT: Monet's moody *Le Parlement* delivers as much heat as a fire in the Georgian fireplace among the icy, cool mirrored walls and modern Mies van der Rohe chairs.

ABOVE: Anne's artwork made Mark's decorating sing. Here, Edgar Degas's *Danseuse attachant son chausson* sits casually on the mantel in Anne's bedroom.

LEFT: A full canopy provides a cozy nest always, but especially when the bed is not anchored to one wall.

CASA DE PILATOS

The Casa de Pilatos, a sixteenth-century palazzo in Seville, Spain, has happily popped up in my life a few times, to lasting effect. It is a combination of Andalusian Mudéjar architecture and decoration blended with Renaissance forms and elements, along with a dash of Gothic flourish added for good measure. Mudéjar architecture is, of course, its own blend of influences resulting from the coexistence of Islamic Moors, Christians, and Jews who lived side by side for about five centuries in Spain, and it is Spanish-specific. It is a melting pot of trajectories pointing every which way that somehow attains harmony and is a maximalist's dream. For anyone interested in such design, the Casa de Pilatos presents an opportunity for a pilgrimage.

In its own way, the special trip that the Hampton girls would take when we each turned sixteen years old was a pilgrimage. We were allowed to pick a destination to travel to with our father, as special father–daughter time. When it was my turn, I picked Spain. This was also the first time my father would visit that beautiful country, so we had a pretty robust tourist schedule. We went to Madrid, Toledo, Seville, and Granada with the understanding that Spain would require, like most places, subsequent trips to ever really know it. My favorite place, along with the Charles V Palace in the Alhambra, the Royal Site of San Lorenzo de El Escorial, and the Royal Tobacco Factory in Seville (made famous by the Bizet opera), was this "casa."

Unlike all the other destinations on the itinerary, the Casa is unique for being relatively small and nestled inside the city center, hidden by a gate. Once you pass through that gate, though, watch out! Like so many spaces that speak to me, it has a symmetrical, structured facade surrounding a central courtyard and is adorned by shapes that any budding neoclassicist would recognize and love. Overlaying those recognizable shapes come Mudéjar carvings, which are byzantine in their complexity. The walls are also peppered with Greek and Roman busts, all surrounded by lush, manicured gardens.

The idea that this house was influenced by the Stations of the Cross and even named for Pontius Pilate is intriguing, but it is made even more interesting by simultaneously displaying the Islamic concept of divine unity. This trip was my first introduction to the notion of the infinite that is expressed in Islamic designs, and here it was, in interlocking geometries covering immense swaths of the facade in carved details and then inside, with multicolored tiles, or azulejos, applied just about anywhere and everywhere. Meant to suggest the unknowability of God's vastness, these endless linear variations are meditative, and they give a new dimension to old loves, like the meandering, endless Greek key. To experience the Casa de Pilatos is to have an intellectually provocative encounter with design, and it is just the right, digestible size to do so, though by no means is the place little.

Thirteen years later, on my honeymoon, Pavlos and I were at a tiny shop by the Gritti Palace that sold Fortuny fabrics in cut yardages. I spied what would become our headboard for our new primary bedroom and went about purchasing it immediately. I likely called Anthony Lawrence-Belfair on the spot to learn the quantity I would need. While we were there, only one other couple was present, which was pretty much all the place could hold beyond its shopkeeper. We struck up a conversation and they were excited to hear tales of our honeymoon. This older, elegant duo was from Seville, Spain. I told them that was where one of my all-time favorite houses was located. When they asked the location and I replied it was the Casa de Pilatos, they told us that it was *their* house! Seriously, what were the chances? I was delighted but also more than a little mortified to be gushing about that

> "To experience the Casa de Pilatos is to have an intellectually provocative encounter with design..."

OPPOSITE: This orange and white paint is but one example of many uses of bold color throughout this Mudéjar masterpiece.

The three loggias were designed by Neapolitan architect Benvenuto Tortello in the 1560s to display a collection of Roman busts and statues acquired by Per Afán Enríquez de Ribera, who inherited Casa de Pilatos from his Uncle Don Fadrique.

house to them, but I got over it and decided it was a happy coincidence.

The Kips Bay Room that I decorated in 2014 at the Villard House (see page 233) was my little tribute to the Casa de Pilatos. I wanted to tackle that enormous amount of pattern and overlay, and it ended up being one of my husband's favorite rooms (and mine, I'll admit) that he has seen of my work. He said to me, "Why can't we do something like that in our house?" Instead of snapping back with "By all means, get me a house like this one and I will," I decided to agree with him and that I'd give myself license to do just that, adding a little more dimension to our new apartment. File that under "Be careful what you wish for," Pavlos.

Although Pavlos and I have been to Spain many times together, we went there on our first architectural trip in 2021, just the two of us. We went to Madrid and Cordova and ended up in Seville for a dear friend's fiftieth birthday. Pavlos's love for the Casa equals mine, and we can't wait to return; next time, lugging the kids.

ABOVE, TOP TO BOTTOM: The niches in the wall were designed specifically to house the classical antiquities collected by Per Afán Enríquez de Ribera during his time serving as Viceroy of Naples (1558–1571) and are the prime example of the classical influences of Casa de Pilatos.

The ornate Mudéjar stucco arches sit atop marble columns. The transition from brick to marble floor along with the addition of the marble statues is another Renaissance addition.

OPPOSITE: The walls are covered in countless polychromed azulejo tiles in Mudéjar motifs. The blue-and-white marble floor replaced modest brick in a later update.

TOP: Bill Blass ignited my passion for helmets, but I must also attribute this marble one depicting Pan for making me the happy helmet aficionado I have become.

ABOVE LEFT: The ceiling in the ceremony room evokes all the wonder and awe of the stars in the skies above.

ABOVE RIGHT: The stairs leading to the winter palace are billed as Seville's first staircase.

OPPOSITE: Here, the detailed relief does the heavy lifting as a departure from the Mudéjar tiles. It should be a surprise to no one that this is a favorite of mine in the Casa de Pilatos.

NEOCLASSICISM IN THE NORTH

One of the greatest influences on all of us and in every realm is the selection of the books we read and to which we have exposure. Once we are in charge of our own libraries (especially our design libraries), our books can become a reaffirmation of what we already know we like. This is true for me as I hunt down and purchase books that show me details that I love and want to catalog for posterity or reference. Maybe that's why other people's libraries can be so exciting. They provide breadth, scope, and information you might otherwise miss, and titles of which you may be entirely ignorant. Learning my trade with the books with which we were required to acquaint ourselves, in addition to other reference sources at our office, obviously has had a lasting influence on my style choices.

Some of the most thumbed-through books at our workplace include the 1975 Jansen monograph, Jonathan Alpert's *Apartments for the Affluent* (a beyond-terrible title, but a great book for illustrating the floor plans of storied New York buildings—pun intended), the 1970 book on David Adler by Richard Pratt, *Les Réussites de la Décoration Française* (both volumes), and more. A title that arrived in 1990 (and thus likely seemed old by the time I became aware of it) was Håkan Groth's magnificent *Neoclassicism in the North: Swedish Furniture and Interiors 1770–1850.* I still experience joy picking up this book and gazing at the splendid photos by Fritz von der Schulenburg. It is currently on my bedside table, but it gets around.

I have been to Sweden a good amount and had already been there before I found this book on the office shelves. As you can imagine, I gravitate to Gustavian design, with the Pavilion at Haga and its interiors by Louis Masreliez as my favorite (the copper tents make my knees weak). King Gustav III, as with so many before and after, was, himself, deeply influenced by his own trips abroad, particularly his rather late grand tour. And, while Versailles was the big inspiration he took away, Gustav also grew up in the aftermath of the discovery of Pompeii, which so drastically shifted much of European taste away from the rococo (which I am not sad about) and straight into the

arms of the more noble and harmonizing styles of ancient Rome. Drottningholm, though baroque, is another obvious favorite and more than justifies Stockholm's reputation at the time as a Paris of the North (which must have enraged his cousin Catherine the Great, with whom he literally went to war).

There are many things I love about Swedish design; especially its pale, watery color palette and its drive to capture all the light it can in a country that is dark for so much of the year. (Although they also have crazy white nights in the summer; I have tumbled out of a Stockholm nightclub at three in the morning in the company of Pavlos and a bunch of our friends, only to be confronted with the sight of our sweaty, over-served appearances in the bright light of day. Yikes!)

The Swedish interpretation of eighteenth-century French design is also captivating. While frequently less ornate, more pared down, and often free of gilding, Gustavian furniture is also somehow more upright and less fussy for those same reasons. Devoid of all that glitters, the Swedish clock and klismos chair ascends to appear as pure sculpture. At the least regal end of its design spectrum, it manages to convey coziness and charm in the face of being so very much designed and buttoned-up. The combination of a humble ticking stripe or a cotton check on a bleached white chair with intricate, Louis XVI–derived carvings is one of which I will never tire. It's definitely an eat-your-cake-and-have-it-too situation.

Groth's book illustrates so well so much of what I love about design that I will never not know where it is in my apartment. It is from the cover of this book that I chose our apartment's prevailing curtain style, and I've used it on many other projects as well. The possession of a good design library is one of the most necessary staples for a

> "Once we are in charge of our own libraries (especially our design libraries), our books can become a reaffirmation of what we already know we like."

OPPOSITE: Decorated in 1782, this bedroom with its floral hand-painted Chinese silk covering the walls, curtains, and furniture allows the graceful lines of the Louis XVI armchairs and commode to shine. It is also the perfect bed alcove that I've always especially loved.

modern-day designer or design enthusiast. Yes, many things are google-able, but we all know that what we see on a book page is ultimately better and more thorough and more satisfying. As my eyes get tired and the fonts seem to get smaller and fuzzier, my library at home has shifted in content. I no longer need to house my fiction or historical biographies in bookcases, as I invariably need them on a device that can enlarge the text size. For a few favorites, my "reading books" are in the cloud. So, books on art, architecture, and decoration have fully taken over. For many, the coffee table book is an object. For me, it's a necessity.

CLOCKWISE FROM ABOVE: Klismos chairs, a Biedermeier table, and Gustavian sofa work beautifully in this late-eighteenth-century salon. In combination, the pieces are a great lesson to us all to keep referring to historic places. • An anteroom of this size and scale is fit for royalty with its French renaissance harp, Louis XVI chairs, and a reproduction of Sergel's *Cupid and Psyche* sculpture. • This bedroom, decorated in the 1770s, boasts family portraits above a table displaying the most beautiful porphyry vases and boxes. • This hall is a celebration of Sweden's 1788 victory over Russia, and a masterpiece of trompe l'œil crown molding and vertical decor lines.

OPPOSITE: The discovery of Pompeii can be felt in every square inch of this splendid grand hall, from the paneled murals and frescoed dado to the porphyry fireplace and klismos sofas and chairs.

CHAPTER 4

EXPANDING WITH 10E + 10D

PAVLOS AND I SPENT our early thirties quite comfortably in 10E. Its eleven-hundred square feet made us feel like we were living in Versailles compared to 7G, which was barely six-hundred square feet. For us both to be in the house at the same time and not see each other—well, that felt very luxurious. With the birth of our twin sons, and our daughter two years later, we were blessed with riches more valuable than gold, and our lives were filled with unimaginable joy, laughter, and exhaustion. That's when we were graced with enough good fortune to purchase 10D, a one-bedroom apartment next door to 10E.

Now that we had three children under the age of two, you might say that 2008 was a time of great change in our family life, but the world outside our home seemed to be spinning faster too. While I was working on floor plans for our reconfigured house and juggling client projects, others less fortunate were facing the effects of a bursting American housing bubble, which dominoed into a huge economic recession that left few unscathed as markets all around the world tumbled. Amid all of this, history was being made: China hosted the summer Olympics for the first time, Google's first version of Chrome was released, and a relatively unknown senator from Illinois was elected the first African American president of the United States.

For me, it would be the first time that the dream shared by all New Yorkers came true. I discovered an extra bedroom behind a closet door. Maybe this dream isn't limited to just New Yorkers . . . Alice visits

OPPOSITE: Looking at the serene palette and clean, orderly lines of this room does not hint at the chaotic reality that the adults were outnumbered by toddlers in this household.

OVERLEAF: Considering my current exuberance for color, I laugh to think that I ever attempted discipline by sticking to a range of neutrals. The blue-glass Louis XIV–style photophores are the only exception to the rule.

Wonderland through a mirror portal while other dimensions are accessed through a wardrobe. But really, sleeping—much less dreaming—during my children's toddler years may have been an overly ambitious feat when my side hustles included multiple product collaborations, speaking engagements, and publishing my first book. All in addition to my "day job," which included decorating New York City pieds-à-terre, forty-thousand-square-foot compounds in the South of France, and a Feadship yacht in Amsterdam, plus designing villas in Beijing. Oh, and I was also on PBS's *This Old House* as the first female cast member and then cohosted the network's show *Find!* with the Keno twins of *Antiques Roadshow* fame.

As Karl Lagerfeld is rumored to have said, "If you want something done, ask a working mother," a twist on Ben Franklin's axiom, "If you want something done, ask a busy person." I cannot attest to the veracity of the modern attribution, but the sentiment is completely true. Mothers who also work outside the home are rarely afforded the luxury of time, so projects are done quickly, efficiently, and correctly from the start (for the most part), because few have it in them to go back and re-do work. The more I had to do, the more I did and continued doing.

RIGHT: By virtue of being an American decorator, I, like some of my peers, have a proclivity for pastiche—such as French antiques and generally neoclassical motifs. I see our eclectic approach to architectural and interior decorating styles as affirming us as perpetual innovators and the birthplace of new art forms, be it jazz or motion pictures.

Just as in our previous bedroom, fully operational curtains could not be used on the windows because of the radiator covers, so I opted for motorized blackout shades concealed by a swagged-and-tassled valance.

URBAN OASIS

With the addition of 10D, baby Kiki moved into the boys' old nursery. Michalis and Markos moved into our old bedroom, and a new principal bedroom was created from the former living room of the apartment next door. The spacious dimensions of our new bedroom inspired me to create a hilltop-like sanctuary where Pavlos and I could retreat each night.

The incredibly high ceilings, normally a boon to any room, posed a design challenge to making our sleeping space cozy and welcoming. A canopy bed could easily solve that problem, but Pavlos was opposed to the idea, thinking it would make the room feel too feminine. So naturally, I had to prove him wrong. I am of the school of thought that believes design features need not be completely feminine or totally masculine.

As our global conversation has become less gendered, I find myself saying *masculine* less and replacing that word with *handsome* because that's really what I mean. So, I set out to create a handsome canopy bed.

I designed a geometric frame to suspend from the ceiling and used gender-neutral textiles to create a tailored look. The woven geometric taupe fabric on the bed curtains and underside of the canopy riffed off the strict 90-degree angles of the frame (right angles are my favorite kind of angle), while the reverse "dry" side of a white chintz on the exterior of the canopy and bed skirt served as a good foil to accentuate the crisp cut of the canopy frame.

To create a look that is at once modern and traditional, I added deeper crown moldings around the room and along the ceiling beams; low wainscoting also added architectural interest. Clean lines were extended to the bookshelves flanking the fireplace, which was updated with a new mantel and a bold black marble surround. I loved the idea of having a fire while lounging in bed, but the reality of a wood-burning fireplace in a light-colored room was none too practical. Oops. This would not be the only time the romance of an idea misled me when designing our bedroom (as you'll learn in the next chapter).

DECORATING
FOR CHILDREN

When I was growing up, my parents allowed us access to all the rooms of our house. There weren't any spaces that were off-limits because of fragile antiques and valuable art. Of course, mishaps occur, like that time my sister, Kate, tried to kick me and the clog on her foot came off. I ducked and the wooden shoe broke the window before landing outside on Park Avenue. Thankfully, we didn't live on a high floor so there wasn't the required velocity to turn the shoe into a deadly projectile. That being said, our parents almost killed us.

There was that other time, in my boy-crazy youth, I was chasing after a handsome magician performing for my birthday, and I crashed into a full-height mirrored dining room screen, causing it to smash into a million shards of glass. Those were bad days for the decor at the Hampton household, but they were rare. Besides, how boring would childhood be without a few broken things? The point is, my parents taught us how to live and mostly behave in spaces appropriate to the setting, and we usually (mostly) abided.

Earlier in my career when working with clients who asked me to round off certain edges to accommodate children, I responded with the same approach my parents used. But then I had two boys and I quickly realized my own bullshit. Humble pie is best served by your own lovable children or with sleep deprivation for those sans offspring.

Our previous bedroom with its cool blue walls worked perfectly for the boys' new bedroom. I realize I said previously that I didn't believe in gendered decorating, but, alas, parenting makes hypocrites of us all and proves Plato's point that "The worst of all deceptions is self-deception." In all seriousness, I love that color, so there was no need to improve upon perfection. The space worked well not only because we didn't have to repaint it, but also because it was large enough to fit two twin beds and most of the accouterments that growing boys require. A row of graphic Robert Indiana numbers in bright colors reflected the vibrancy and liveliness of the inhabitants' personalities. The decorating in that room was limited to these prints and a globe because, as any parent can attest, children's interests change just as quickly as they do. To provide fodder for sweet dreams and life beyond the apartment walls, I plastered a world

map on the ceiling. That map proved to be a harbinger of things to come, decoratively speaking.

Clearly, Pavlos and I are obsessed with maps, and that brightly colored one was the first step in a love affair of decorating with maps of all types. We also thought it was important for the boys (and then our daughter) to know at some point that their place in the world was not rooted in just the modern mecca of New York, but also in Greece, the ancient birthplace of Western civilization.

With the boys' room largely settled, Kiki's room came together nearly as easily. Having the basics of her room in a muted color allowed us the flexibility to change up the "soft" furnishings, such as bed linens, to suit her ever-evolving tastes. I don't know why, but it seems many little girls between the ages of two and five go through a pink princess phase, regardless of their New York parents' all-black everyday wardrobe. This is a case where nature definitely won over nurture. That said, I was happy not to do too much of a nursery-theme design. It was really just a placeholder.

ABOVE AND OPPOSITE, TOP: The first iteration of the boys' room had two beds, side by side, while the second featured bunk beds that converted into desks.

OPPOSITE, BOTTOM: For the current version, I commissioned Dean Barger to paint this idealized view of Michelangelo's Piazza del Campidoglio, set atop the Capitoline Hill, a symbol of eternity for Romans. .

TRAVEL IS THE BEST TEACHER

There are enough Vatican references in my house now that one might mistake me for a Catholic. The answer to why a nice Quaker like me is obsessed with the Vatican and its assorted paraphernalia is simple: Some of the best times in my life—as a child with my parents and now as an adult with my own children—were spent going to Rome or touring churches. Nearly every square inch of Rome calls to mind an exquisite sensation via sight, sound, smell, taste, and touch. Besides, I further justify the zeal of my decorating choices by the fact that I have a Greek husband who was raised in Rome. Pavlos not only grew up there, but his father was also the ambassador to the Holy See itself, and Pavlos even met Pope John Paul on a couple of occasions.

As I mentioned in *The Language of Interior Design*, I had visited the Pantheon, Parthenon, and Buckingham Palace by the time I was twelve. No doubt, experiencing the great houses and palaces of ancient empires imprinted upon my impressionable mind what it meant to live in extraordinary surroundings. My visits to palaces at Versailles and Blenheim convinced me these were the places that read glamor and otherworldliness, far more than anything Hollywood could serve up—with the exception of James Bond movies.*

Another house museum in Paris, the Musée Nissim de Camondo, left a strong impression on me. These historic residences—palaces really—have been kept impeccably, and moving through the rooms, even though they're roped off, gives me the feeling of living in them. When I visit, I'm completely transported back to that specific time and place in my imagination. The memories of going there as a child with my family, and more recently with my husband as an adult, are magical. It's the same kind of feeling one might get when watching a cooking show and they're making a favorite dish from your childhood; in your mind's eye, you are immediately transported back to your family's kitchen, surrounded by familiar tastes and comforting smells.

When I see something that reminds me of trips to the Musée Nissim de Camondo or, more recently, the Palazzo Colonna in Rome, I'm giddy with the joy of a kid on summer break. I remember the incredible meals

I've had and the luxury of staying in hotels, which might be my favorite thing ever. I'm of that generation when nice hotels still provided their own stationery and postcards at their writing desks. A few times, I would even mail postcards home to friends from trips abroad. The disappearance has made them even more charming in my memory.

So many elements from those early family vacations are etched into my memory on a tremendous scale. To create these moments for my own children is a sublime delight. To stay in a hotel, eat foreign foods expertly prepared, wear different clothes (for me, an event in and of itself), and see magnificent places always spoke and still speaks to me emotionally. I am equally in love with the fantasy of palace living as I am in coming home and having McDonald's, the American that I am. Currently, I can claim only the latter, but my photo collection of Massimo Listri from Celia Rogge gets me as close as possible to the former.

As an adult, I've traveled a lot for both work and pleasure and am possibly the only person in the world who is still sometimes elated at an airport. The prospect of traveling fills me with a joy connected to those childhood trips. Unlike most every other human on Earth, I love being at the airport because of the promise and excitement of going somewhere. The thrill I feel when the plane begins its descent and I look out the window to see the little lights is the same I felt when I rode a Ferris wheel for the first time—and it looks like it too. I have long held the goal to work in as many towns, countries, and continents as possible. After twenty-plus years of pursuing just that, I am still in love with travel and learning about new places. I have a lot of terrain to cover still, and I relish this challenge.

---

*I've seen every single Bond movie many times and I love them all so much; my ringtone is the 007 theme song. My first Bond movie was *The Spy Who Loved Me,* which was set in Egypt.

OPPOSITE: The exterior of the Altes Museum in Berlin was designed by my favorite architect, Karl Friedrich Schinkel.

WALKING THE FINE LINE BETWEEN COLLECTION AND CLUTTER

With all the shifts in the world and in our family life from 2008 to 2013, leaving our living room largely unchanged came as a relief. This isn't to say that I didn't continue feathering our nest in the living room. My predisposition is to find and gather things. I fall in love with fossilized mud, marble spheres, obelisks, miniature ruins, and Roman helmets and then I want five of each at minimum. But there's a point at which I just have to keep my eye on myself, beyond the fact that there is now a distinct lack of tabletop space. Sometimes, when I don't want to scratch the itch of retail therapy, I'll clean or rearrange my collections. We can't all be like Sir John Soane with our collections—would that we could.

If your collections verge on the point of magpie madness, I suggest you first have a Marie Kondo moment to gauge whether certain objects still have a connection to your heart. Does the item still bring a smile to your face when you remember its provenance, or is it something nice from an old romance that soured? Or perhaps it was something you bought that you thought was cute at one point but your tastes have evolved. Change is inevitable, and your collections should reflect your own growth as a person. I'm not recommending that you throw out everything, but instead edit the things that are filler so the true gems in your collection can shine. Be at peace, as I am for the most part, having been a stalwart steward of the object. Then, let it go.

When I recently hung two of Ashley Hicks's paintings in my living room, I realized that the collections on the little temple bookcases below them were overdone so I started pulling away some of my marble straight edges and relocating them to other tablescapes. I took out some things that were originally an expression of where I wanted to go; now that I had arrived at that place, I could release them into the wild. Ashley's paintings of the military trophies on a background of trompe l'oeil porphyry were just too good to be pulled down by "stuff."

Once you have all the pieces you truly love, arranging the items en masse on a bookshelf or a tabletop makes a dramatic statement. Carefully composed collections can act as a three-dimensional tour through history–cum–art installation. When arranging your tablescapes, keep in mind the basic tenets of good design: contrast, proportion, color, and balance. For example, if you're arranging a collection of framed photographs, consider contrasting dark and light woods or polished and brushed metals. How do the individual pieces relate to one another and as a whole to the rest of the room? Is there enough color contrast from the surface or wall to allow the collection to pop? If you are keeping things monochrome, have you let another color creep in? Asking these questions helps to secure the goal: Keep the eyes engaged with the story you are trying to tell. Very few things bring me more joy than arranging these portals to another time and place. In fact, my tabletop displays are among my favorite things in my apartment—total decorator porn.

LETTING GO OF PERFECTION

With great patience and some difficulty, Pavlos and I continued to live in 10E + 10D among our tazzas and urns, bergères and busts. Some pieces, however, were sacrificed to the angry gods to smite me for my insatiable love of books and architectural models. We lived here until Kiki was five years old, and with the last of our babies having graduated from kindergarten, our house and interiors would level up also.

CLOCKWISE FROM TOP LEFT: Obelisks, tempiettos, urns, friezes, and marble samples—these are my particular talismans.

The specific way that I lay out my tablescapes is influenced by my love of strict compositions and my fondness for trompe l'œil rack paintings that spool over canvases, like the painting in my mom's living room on Park Avenue.

Molded-lion paperweights sit atop my favorite books.

KARL FRIEDRICH SCHINKEL

In 2004, right before my bunion surgery (as I would describe it) or just after Greece won the Euro soccer competition (as my husband would describe it), Pavlos and I joined two of our favorite people on a jaunt to Berlin to sightsee. I had been to Germany once before, for a wedding in Bonn, but this was my first time in Berlin, and I promptly lost my mind. *Unter den Linden.*

Of course, I knew of Schinkel. What do you take me for, a philistine?! But, this was my first time clapping my eyes on his buildings in real life. Actually, that must be a lie. I surely saw the Alexander Nevsky chapel at Peterhof in Saint Petersburg as a young 'un, but I must have been chewing my cuticles and shooting dark looks at my parents while we were discussing who was the architect. I was a teenager then, after all.

Walking to Museum Island and around Berlin, seeing all the buildings of this astonishing architect/urban designer/furniture designer/set designer was a revelation. To this day, I do not understand why we aren't raving about Schinkel all the time. Again, my reverence for nineteenth-century classicism reared its head. Alongside my eternal love of American Greek revival buildings of the 1840s and my love of Parisian city planning—as started in the second half of the 1800s by Haussmann—I now slotted in total devotion to early-nineteenth-century Schinkel.

The Altes Museum in Berlin, characterized by monumental simplicity, is replete with an interior rotunda modeled after the Pantheon in Rome. This and the Romisch Bader, nestled in the countryside, adorned with caryatids lifted from the Acropolis, and sprinkled around a bathing niche, are just two examples of Schinkellian genius. Everything is over the top as well as buttoned-up, equal parts academic architecture and the implementation of fantasy.

> "I had been to Germany once before, for a wedding in Bonn, but this was my first time in Berlin, and I promptly lost my mind."

The apogee of all this love came to a head upon viewing the equal parts of the magnificent and human-scale Charlottenhof Villa, off to the side of Sanssouci Palace, in Potsdam. If you are a decorator, you know Charlottenhof, whether you can name it or not. It is, of course, the location of the most famous blue-and-white-striped room on Earth (and mother to many, many more done in loving homage to it). It is a tented campaign room, designed for the future king Frederick William IV when he was still crown prince. Although it clearly refers to ancient Roman bivouacs, it somehow remains shockingly modern.

The Villa defies its colorful, Pompeii-inspired chromatic drama by somehow maintaining the appearance of a strict, formal Germanic villa nonetheless. (I'd like to take a minute to propose a new word for your delectation: *architeutonic.* Yay!) It's all the more dramatic for residing next door to the elaborate, baroque Sanssouci Palace. Indeed, if Sanssouci can lay claim to the word *insouciance,* Charlottenhof can lay claim to *ceremoniousness.* And, I love it all the more for it!

I raise my glass and tip my helmet to Schinkel, whose array of proximate buildings always seems to suggest a manicured parade for an upright citizenry looking to ancient Greece for its twin examples of idealism and intellectual rectitude.

OPPOSITE: The dome ceiling of the neoclassical masterpiece that is the Altes Museum on Museum Island is decorated with red-and-gold coffers depicting signs of the zodiac, a variety of winged fairies, and rosettes alongside Giotto's arena chapel, inspiration for later ceiling designs in my own home.

TOP AND ABOVE: I love how strict Schinkel's designs are, especially in Charlottenhof. The graphic quality of his rooms, loaded with high-contrast decoration, achieve, for me, the perfect balance between richness and stricture. Let's talk about the regal scale of the furniture in this very demurely scaled villa. Its counterintuitive combination is the result of a master at his work. Especially powerful is his combination of elevated shapes: curved niches aside rectangular artworks, balanced perfectly by a red studded door.

ABOVE: Charlottenhof Villa is ArchiTeutonic design exemplified by Schinkel's vibrant color story in the strict lines of formal Germanic architecture harkening back to ancient Rome.

OVERLEAF: One of the most referenced rooms in design history lives in Charlottenhof Villa, built and decorated from 1826 to 1829. It is the tent room, a blue-and-white tour de force.

ABOVE: In an otherwise humbly sized room in Charlottenhof, Schinkel deploys bold color and drama to imbue the space with pomp. These circumstances betray his expertise as a set designer.

OPPOSITE, TOP: .A lesser-known view of this iconic room. Schinkel manages to elevate a simple slipcover into high art. His very tight hold on each detail he renders is what heightens the effect of his design. His love of stagecraft couldn't be more apparent.

OPPOSITE, BOTTOM: The placement of such a famous bronze sculpture (*Boy with Thorn*) depicting a boy removing a thorn from his foot, seems a sly reference to the fact that a bath is the perfect location for such intimate ablutions.

ABOVE: Incorporating some of the recent architectural findings from the excavation of Pompeii and Herculaneum is a mix of an idealized fifteenth-century Italian country house and an ancient Roman bathhouse. It is easy to see that Schinkel was also a skilled set designer—his sense of drama is irresistible.

OPPOSITE, TOP: Perhaps it is the deep-seated romance and idealism present in Schinkel's work on Romische Bader (the Roman baths) that resonate so deeply with me.

OPPOSITE, BOTTOM: As if Charlottenhof wasn't already a sufficient homage to the gods of Pompeii, after its completion, then crown prince Frederick William IV commissioned Schinkel to build Romische Bader (the Roman baths). In the atrium sits a decorative bathtub made of green jasper.

2012 KIPS BAY SHOW HOUSE: WEST SIDE STORY

In 1973, I was only two years old when supporters of the Kips Bay Boys and Girls Club began inviting celebrated interior decorators to transform a townhouse as a fundraiser for New York City after-school programming. Now, nearly fifty years after its inception, the Kips Bay Decorator Show House is an institution in and of itself and a must-see for any design enthusiast. I am proud to now be the Show House's co-chair alongside Jamie Drake.

Because my father was so often invited to participate, the Kips Bay Show House became a part of our annual traditions much like Easter in the spring or snow days in the winter. When I was in the third grade, my father arranged for my entire class to take a field trip to see the show house, which was a little weird as a field trip but totally wonderful. For as long as I can remember, my family has been involved in this incredibly important cause.

I was first invited to participate in this prestigious showcase in 1999, the year after my father died. The stairway landing that I designed was elegant and classical, intended to basically telegraph to the industry and anyone else that the firm Mark Hampton was in the somewhat capable hands of this twenty-seven-year-old decorator. I hoped to create continuity by producing a room that reflected the firm's history.

More than a decade would pass before I felt ready to expand what I wanted to say as Alexa Hampton, not just Mark Hampton's daughter. The 2012 Kips Bay Show House was particularly special because Bunny Williams, David Kleinberg, and Brian J. McCarthy collaborated on a room to honor Albert Hadley, who had died at the age of ninety-one that year. Furthermore, I was in great company—the invited decorators included Charlotte Moss, Thom Filicia, Brian del Toro, and David Scott, among a slew of other wonderful contributors. Although I hadn't done a room for Kips Bay in a long time, I knew one thing was sure: I could not do a show house and not totally go for it, so flex I would.

> "I wanted to realize a fantastical bedroom that was no longer embarrassed by its exuberant glamor."

Departing from years past, the 2012 Show House was not in a brownstone or a townhouse but a completely brand-new West Side skyscraper. Since the building was so modern, I thought it would be fun to go against the grain and contrarily produce a traditional prewar bedroom. Also, from a practical business standpoint, I wanted purchasers of newly built high-rise apartments to understand that they had options. They need not adhere to modern interiors to match the exterior. Therefore, my call to arms would be to zig when circumstances zagged.

I created what I think is a beautifully layered boudoir with a canopy bed. The duo-chrome room had charcoal-lacquered walls and a silver ceiling. Playing off the theme of high contrast, I paired rich, soft fabrics against the very slick, lacquered walls and furniture. It was moody and sexy, and I loved decorating every inch of that bedroom. The dark walls were sure to make an impact. At the time of that third-grade field trip to the show house, I saw my father's room was a chocolate-brown library with white upholstery; this bedroom was a wink to that.

I have always enjoyed being my parents' daughter (or my father's daughter in the world of design). That said, I absolutely enjoy subverting those preconceived notions with a dirty mouth that would make a sailor blush. Usually, that instinct is curbed when working, but at this point in my career and personal life, I was shedding some of the constraints of polite society's notions of propriety from me. I wanted to realize a fantastical bedroom that was no longer embarrassed by its exuberant glamor.

OPPOSITE: To create a sumptuous feel for this bedroom from top to bottom, I called in all my favorite collaborators. I borrowed the circa 1890 Amritsar antique carpet from Beauvais; the taffeta curtains were made by Anthony Lawrence-Belfair, while many of the accessories on the desk came from Niall Smith (see page 61); the desk itself came from Florian Papp.

CLOCKWISE FROM TOP LEFT: The sculptural scrolls on the arms of this uniquely caned bergère, with its rich navy velvet upholstery, worked perfectly with velvet on the slippers. • I can't think of a texture more plush than fur (faux, naturally—or unnaturally as the case may be). • Details matter, such as the talons on this Empire flower next to the velvet slippers of my imagined Proustian resident. • The celadon lamp was just the perfect color to pair with the paintings, especially the large one of the Colosseum. Objets Plus and Niall Smith are to thank.

ABOVE: A study of contrasts in textures: lacquered walls and silver
ceilings paired with the delicate hand of the fur bedspread and
dreamy canopy and curtains.

The tension between curves and straight lines plays out between the swag and jabot valance versus the box pleats in the canopy and bed skirt, as well as on the shapes of the Moroccan-flavored linen embroidery.

Decorating this bedroom was absolutely thrilling because it was fun and enjoyable just for the sake of pleasure, not because I expected the room to perform for a particular kind of customer. Participating in a show house like this can be a marketing ploy as well as a charitable effort, a way for decorators to telegraph to the public their prowess and expertise. I wanted to just have fun with it for no other reason than because I liked it. I knew it was not in the realm of reality that any client would ask me to decorate something as salacious or louche. Dark lacquered walls and a reflective bedroom ceiling—hold on to your wigs, ladies! Choosing to go traditional in a contemporary setting was one thing, but allowing myself to be completely unfettered with creativity was what I needed. If I did this type of room only once in my lifetime, it would have been completely satisfying.

When one of my designer friends walked through the room with me, he was wonderfully complimentary and then said he wished decorators would do something this dramatic for High Point. After about a millisecond of reflection, I realized there was no good reason for me not to "swing for the fences" when at the Furniture Market. The success of that room marked a turning point for me to be bolder in my uncommissioned work, perhaps much in the same way that a life-affirming experience gained through participation in one of the wonderful programs offered by the Kips Bay Boys and Girls Club might affect a young mind. Decorating for the Kips Bay Show House really does prove how good it feels to give and participate.

RIGHT, TOP: The small, black ebonized statuette of a Renaissance figure sits beside bibelots of ancient ruins.

RIGHT, BOTTOM: The sepia tones of the historical prints lent by Florian Papp Gallery harmonize with the shiny charcoal walls.

OPPOSITE: A crisp white seemed a natural color choice for the headboard and bedding in a room so dark and moody. Having the inside bed curtains in a soft embroidery eases the transition to the rest of the room.

JOHN SOANE

I first went to England and France when I was six or eight—who can remember? One of the highlights of that trip was visiting the house museum of the architect of the Bank of England, Sir John Soane. The three connected townhouses on Lincoln's Inn Fields in Holborn, London, spoke to me on an immediate, visceral level. While I had been going to museums my whole short life (frequently unwillingly), this was unlike any museum I had ever seen, and it remains that wondrous way to me even now. It in no way conforms to what a museum "should" look like. There is no particular direction to take once you are inside, and there is no final destination. It is all experience and it is all simultaneous and it keeps folding back on itself like an unwieldy, hungry ouroboros. It is as though some madman with no measure of self-control went on many wonderful adventures and brought back everything he could. In fact, that is a pretty good summation of events; unnuanced but evocative.

Seeing archaeological findings prior to visiting Sir John Soane's Museum (and afterward, if I'm honest) can be quite a dry experience. I have come late to the party as far as loving statues is concerned. While I obviously adore them now, I find observing single statues isolated with nothing around them but tomb-like silence, while striking, can be stifling. That singular objectification of a figure in search of a context lacks romance, to say the least. In the museum, the feeling is equal to entering a life-size advent calendar—everything you open has a little magical surprise behind it. When you step into the residence and workplace of this ingenious Regency architect and connoisseur, you are transported into a playground of sorts.

Soane tried to amplify his surfaces to support the endlessness of his accumulations. On top of that, his collections spill onto different levels. Interior balconies gaze down upon an excavation-like space, replete with a sarcophagus. His use of skylights throughout was a creative trick to combat the lack of light that is endemic to English row houses and the gloomy gray weather so common

> "It is as though some madman with no measure of self-control went on many wonderful adventures and brought back everything he could."

there. And his employment of convex bullseye mirrors to direct light into the dimness of the deep interiors is nothing short of genius, and a signature of his. While it would be a few years yet before I saw Indiana Jones place the headpiece atop the staff of the fictional Amun-Ra, the magic was no less cinematic for me upon seeing the sarcophagus of Seti in the Soane's Museum. The only thing that could have made it better would have been the addition of Harrison Ford. Han Solo was my jam.

Along with oil paintings, a limitless array of renderings of projects both real and imagined sits alongside the tens of thousands of other things that Sir John Soane acquired. The richness of the display combined with the virtuosity of the artworks leaves me speechless. It is a treasure hunt walking through each room because of the unique space and invention present in every square inch of these townhouses—a terminal velocity of things there. The sheer quantity of items in that given space is a glut in a way that speaks to me, as a glutton of great design. It's exuberant and abundant. This density bears the weight of gravity pressing on it, but somehow it is never crushed beneath its heft. Displayed in such a manner, it beckons to a professional tourist and, in this case, a professional design tourist.

While my apartment is in no way capital "S" Soanian, it takes little imagination to connect the dots showing that I am a fan of the museum. I have my architectural friezes (one of which hailed from the Soane shop), and there are wonderful plasters that I have collected along the way. Some have come from another master, Peter Hone (don't even get me started on his rooms), via Pentreath & Hall, while others are from antiques stores around the country and the globe, thanks to late-night forays on the internet.

OPPOSITE: The ingenuity of John Soane's spatial layering is nowhere more apparent than in these hinged paneled walls, which display row after row of paintings on the front side and back.

ABOVE: After swinging open several hinged panels of paintings, one is further rewarded with a little shrine dedicated to Shakespeare. Why not?

LEFT: The Dome holds the bulk of Soane's marbles and plasters of busts, architectural fragments, reliefs, and anything with a form that was pleasing to his eye.

OPPOSITE, TOP TO BOTTOM: The Pompeiian red walls are not the only thing evocative of ancient Rome here; the rooms are rich with vases, paintings, busts, and books.

Mirrors behind the large-scale portraits make this already large room grander, but it's the use of convex bullseye mirrors that are Soane's signature trick. Here, they are deployed to the corners to direct light and draw the eye to the busts mounted high.

Soane loved to deep dive into rich combinations not only with color but also with shapes and angles. Where the books are staunchly upright, the three graceful arches and his collection of ancient Greek and Roman vases contrast to create an engrossing dialogue.

Another thing I always wanted as a result of my early exposure to the Soane museum was to have secrets that could be discovered among the humble objects of my diurnal life. (Alert: I misidentified the word *diurnal* on my GREs all those years ago, to my horror. It is only right that I casually use it here to alleviate my shame.) Mostly, I have achieved this with a double false bookcase that can close off the living and dining rooms. In other places, a jib door or two, or three, lend a little magic. The crux of it was that I wanted a little wonder to call my own. No grown-up dwelling can be complete without it.

ABOVE: Another one of Soane's architectural magic effects is his use of cantilevered stairs, which gives one the feeling of floating in time and space.

OPPOSITE, CLOCKWISE FROM TOP LEFT: Corinthian columns line the path to a life-size reproduction of *Apollo Belvedere* in the dome room. • Marble or plaster, original or reproduced, it didn't matter. To Soane, the only value was whether the form delighted him. • Room after room, layer after layer, there is evidence of Soane's skill for collecting and displaying items together in undisputed harmony. • Each item on display is as exactly as placed at the time of Soane's death in 1837. Even in death, he (or, at least, the marble bust of him on the left) surveys his vast collection of antiquities.

CHAPTER 5

LAYING DOWN ROOTS WITH

10E + 10D + 10C

INSPIRED AFTER WATCHING *Miracle on 34th Street*, my then-seven-year-old son Michalis asked Santa for a little more space. The stars must have been aligned the night that Michalis made his wish in 2013, just as they were decades earlier when Sister Parish overheard my father being interviewed for an internship and, after he left, insisted he be hired because his voice sounded just like her late brother's. Perhaps it was also lucky stars that led Gaby and me to find 12C against the odds. And surely it was good fortune again when 10D became available just before Kiki was born. I don't know the provenance of the Hampton–Papageorgiou's odd luck, but I cannot deny the serendipitous blessings that have visited my family as Michalis's wish came true that Christmas—creating the opportunity to expand and re-create our apartment one last time.

A key to an adjacent apartment was delivered by Santa (Pavlos) under our proverbial tree. When Pavlos

and I first moved into the building, we weren't sure how long we'd be staying, so we had avoided making big (and costly) changes. With the ample square footage that the addition of 10C's new two-bedroom apartment afforded us, I knew we could stay here and our roots could grow. So, I set out to design a forever house for us like where I grew up and where my mother still lives.

Designing a new floor plan kept me up most nights with sketching, sketching, and more sketching. The new apartment would house a living room, a renovated kitchen, a principal bedroom suite, and two principal baths, so Pavlos could finally pursue his cherished dream of not having to share that space with me anymore. Our

OPPOSITE: The tablescape in the entryway leaves no mystery to what I treasure: fantasy scenes of ancient Roman ruins and their artifacts.

former living room would become a family room, while my former bedroom would transform into a dining room befitting the Irish Regency dining table that Pavlos gave me years long ago. We would also address the long-neglected bathrooms and kitchens (there were five in total) and air conditioning situations in this renovation.

In the years since we expanded our footprint, the apartment has become a celebration of our adulthood. I could not have had a place like this when I was younger for a variety of reasons. I didn't truly know my own opinions and, quite frankly, I didn't have the money. It took time, contemplation, and experience to crystallize what I wanted to do. Also, the world and life keep changing, so we have had to adapt. For example, my little antique rosewood writing desk in the window of the living room appeared in 2021 when the coronavirus pandemic demanded we all work from home. Its addition, even though caused by need, absolutely enriched the room. Function sometimes does benefit form.

New York City in the spring of 2020 at the onset of COVID-19 hitting the United States was an "unprecedented" time (dear reader, I, too, am so tired of hearing that word, but by its very definition I have no other option from which to choose). The impact of the pandemic is vast and still unfolding years afterward, and I can't even begin to scratch the surface of its widespread effects.

For my family that March, we were scared and unnerved like everyone else by the nonstop blare of ambulance sirens, and we recognized how lucky we were. The children and I were very fortunate to have the newer side of the apartment to occupy while Pavlos was quarantined for a week in the original parts awaiting a COVID test outcome. Once a negative result came back, we all packed up and decamped to Southampton, where we stayed for a little over a year. It was the longest span of time we had ever been separated from the apartment since first moving there in 2000. During our time away, I pined for it and missed all its idiosyncratic qualities, which I find so charming. I missed the views, the plumbing (our water pressure!), the smell, the mahogany doors. I am not so terminally unique as to escape the trite sentiment of "absence makes the heart grow fonder," and I knew that when we returned, I would fervently shower love and attention upon our home with a renewed sense of vigor.

In 52 Weeks of Design, a project where, every week, I celebrate a different designer that I admire, I speak with

other decorators about all sorts of topics touching upon our line of business, including how we know when a client project is done. We'll almost always have a lasting relationship with our beloved clients, and we'll be there whenever they need us, but we detach emotionally when we finally hand over the keys. If you are a decorator of your own home, however, we are living in our projects, and it can feel like it's never done. Sometimes that's a blessing. Sometimes it's a definite hazard. In my youth, my mother would always tell me to be careful when I was sketching. She told me that there was a point where I would overwork my pencil drawing and I needed to watch for it. As with drawing, you can overshoot in your designs, and I'm aware that I'm teetering on that edge with my collections. Thankfully, this has been reined in for me because I have run out of surfaces.

ABOVE: The gilded laurel wreath on this ebonized medallion of Caesar in profile, brings a glittering warm contrast against the pale, shimmery Gracie wallpaper.

OPPOSITE: The addition of this rosewood desk came about as a consequence of the initial COVID-19 lockdown when we all needed more desktops. We have kept it in its place to hold assorted beloved objects (the small photo of my father; and the larger one of my father in front of the Acropolis).

OPENING GAMBIT

Even those with a cursory understanding of interior design can appreciate the importance of an entryway. It's a home's opening salvo, and we all know how influential a first impression is. My foyer serves as an area to greet people as they enter my house, of course, and, less excitingly, as a staging area to unpack our bags, which we often do (for better or worse, who's to say; it just is), after we travel.

With eleven doors in our entry, between closets and passageways, it is essentially the fulcrum of the apartment, and it was particularly challenging to decorate because it had to serve as the device by which I connect all the rooms, by color, by sensibility, by location, all of it. I love considering the psychological ways that any apartment design works on a person. For example, I initially used mahogany doors for passage doors and jib doors to subtly cue when doors should not be walked through. That way, people who are visiting subconsciously know how to move through the apartment with an unspoken sense of where they should or should not go. I love a theory that threads the needle and makes sense of the space.

Now, here's the part where I make an exception to the rule: In the latest revamp, I switched out a hand-painted, silver landscape wallpaper by Gracie for a new hand-painted Gracie paper with bold blues and greens, depicting maps from the Vatican map gallery. The colors of the land and sea in the new wallpaper speak more to the rooms next to which it lives. To better showcase this new wallpaper, I converted two mahogany passage doors into jib doors, which are symmetrically located. One leads to the bar and the other to the kitchen, and both are on either side of the front door, so the parity works together. Before this alteration, visitors sometimes had trouble finding their way out.

Once you are through the front door and in the entry hallway, you are faced with the living room on the left and the dining room on the right. In between these two doors is one of my favorite tablescapes: Blue-glass Louis XIV–style photophores bookend a delightfully symmetrical display of Roman emperor plasters atop an ebonized Egyptian-accented Biedermeier chest of drawers, itself flanked by a matching pair of fantastical Empire chairs showcasing the splayed wings of griffins. This vignette serves as a wild amuse-bouche for the Hampton–Papageorgiou tasting menu of rooms to come.

ABOVE: A Paestum-like fantasy temple sits atop a lucite plinth.

OPPOSITE: I love the blue-glass photophores so much that I had to give them pride of placement in the entryway alongside the Trajan and Nerva bookends from Cove Landing, which I've had since Pavlos and I lived alone in 10E.

Acquiring architectural models and maps will always be my shopping Achilles' heel.

When it comes to symmetry, I love the balance of pairs. I also love how powerful a moment of purposeful asymmetry can be to dispel a Noah's Ark effect.

DINING ROOM MELTING POT

The dining room, most fittingly, represents a harmonious medley of design traditions, styles, materials, and eras that I find most intoxicating. Bringing a myriad of decorative elements that I love together while also honoring the desires and wishes of my family have never been easier to accomplish than in this room. Two of the items on Pavlos's renovation wish list were fulfilled in the dining room. He wanted a green dining room (done) and he wanted a home with maps, so I gave him that in spades.* And, of course, I had to design a room equal to that aforementioned gorgeous mahogany regency table (when it dutifully served as a writing desk in the library/office of 10E, pre-children.)

In the dining room's earlier incarnation as the principal bedroom, crown molding, neoclassical bookcases, and other architectural elements were already in place. In this renovation, I added decoration to the dado here and in the living room, which is purposely low to amplify the height of the ceilings. So instead of raising the height of the chair rail in a room with high ceilings (as seems to be a prevailing trend), I emphasize the ceiling height by consciously lowering the chair rail. The wainscoting on the dado is not actually made of tile—it's my Mongiardino moment. It is wallpaper designed by myself and the ingenious Chuck Fischer, buoyed by our success with the wallpaper designs we did for my 2014 Kips Bay Room, also known as the Moroccan Room (see pages 233 to 239). We massaged the colors of a historic tile pattern for a mosaic that would complement the dark green paint that I had selected for the walls.

The rest would just be a matter of decor (indeed!). A short list of regions represented in this room include British plaid tablecloth over the Irish Regency table with dining chairs covered in American textiles; a French sideboard; Biedermeier stools; Irish matting; ancient Greco-Roman busts, statues, and fragments; French Aptware urns; Arabesque mosaic wainscoting; and, bringing it all together, antique maps. Once I embraced Pavlos's desire for maps, I needed to select a colorful option to be centrally positioned. The flanking plaster friezes and a pair

of maps of northern and southern Greece lacked color. So, I went on to find the perfect image file of an antique map of Greece in the Library of Congress. My beloved framers at J. Pocker had it printed on heavy linen rag paper, folded it tightly, and crumpled it some. Then, to finish it off, they had tea poured on it. Voilà, instant "antique" map, which is framed and hung above the sideboard.

A bit more stagecraft appears in the bookcases adjacent to the windows. Here, I wanted to make the most of the light from the windows and create a passage to the living room, affording some much-needed circulation between the spaces. We carved into what had been an existing bookcase to forge an opening. Working with my contractor S. Donadic, Inc., and my draftsperson Dip-Min Yuen, we figured out how we could reconcile that opening. We used Harmon hinges to install a slim pair of doors on the dining and living room sides. These hinges allow doors to lie flat when opened, creating a flat wall. We wallpapered over those doors with a leather wallpaper and, finally, used a glue gun and faux-leather book spines (we did not gut real books, which would have been sacrilegious) to create the appearance of genuine bookcases on each side when the doors are closed. When the doors are open, the book-lined tunnel they seemingly create is a satisfying (if head-scratching) illusion of an impossible physical reality.

In the most recent refresh, I collaborated with Gracie wallpaper on a new hand-painted ceiling treatment inspired by the Arena (Scrovegni) Chapel in Padua, Italy, famously conceived by Giotto, which has an ultramarine vaulted ceiling with gold stars and medallions of saints orbiting the Virgin Mary. At the time it was painted, the ultramarine pigment, made of lapis lazuli, was as expensive, if not more so, than gold, and everything about the chapel is, to this day, exuberant and thrilling. The idea of referencing this ceiling to put atop my green dining room was too exciting to pass up, though it would need further secular adaptation. The orbiting medallions in our version have been filled not with saints but astrological

---

*Pavlos's other two wishes in the new apartment were a Japanese toilet, which he got, and a venting grill, which I could not give him because of NYC Department of Buildings regulations. (Sorry, love, you know I would if I could.)

OPPOSITE: In a recent refresh, I designed host chairs (a term my father forbade but that is useful, nonetheless) with trapunto quilting of our initials, HP.

This boldly decorated dining room is a good match for the colorful conversations my friends and family have had around the Irish Regency table.

symbols that tie into the signs of our extended family and friends: Sagittarius, Aquarius, Virgo, and Libra.

And while the dining room's electric-blue ceiling is a heavenly topper to an otherwise strictly composed space, complementing the wall's colors, there was no way on Earth (pun!) that I was going to put that color atop my soothing off-white and russet-toned living room. There, we swapped out the blue for a soft glazed cream background that allowed the gold stars to land a bit more smoothly, and in this room are the four signs of the five members of this household: Gemini, Taurus, Scorpio, and Leo. Someday I am going to have to contend with the fact that the apartment has left out Capricorn, Pisces, Aries, and Cancer. But not today, dear reader.

ABOVE: The columns upon which sit the Aptware urns were updated from 7G to include fluting for more linear interest. Arranging the fragments and busts at different heights keeps my eye moving and engaged. I bought the marble foot for Pavlos when he broke his own playing tennis; more feet have followed. Collecting is that much more fun when you don't take yourself too seriously.

RIGHT: Above the fireplace hangs a Massimo Listri interior portrait of a room at the Vatican, which has a room-expanding optical illusion to it.

RIGHT, TOP: Feathers have been used for ornamentation since prehistoric times all around the world. And nothing delights me more than to see them on a helmet.

RIGHT, BOTTOM: When I look at this 2015 photo of the dining room, I see a need for more drama (hello, ceilings)—more busts, statues, plasters, and my MVPs: colored lamp shades! I also swapped the tablecloth for a purple plaid, and the chairs at the table's head and foot needed to be recovered with monogrammed green leather—just because.

OPPOSITE: I love how the blue Gracie ceiling, featuring Sagittarius in this photo, goes so gracefully with the colors of the wainscoting.

The coral klismos chair (at left) is incredibly comfortable—no wonder the design has been in use since antiquity. This one is from my collection for Hickory Chair.

LIVING ROOM BALANCING ACT

My love of exuberance probably stems from having absorbed via osmosis all the pomp and circumstance intrinsic to the many Catholic churches that I have visited throughout my life. With so much time spent looking at all the pageantry, it seems practically preordained that the gravitas and sobriety of neoclassicism's starkly beautiful architecture and design also enchant me (you know, to keep the balance of the universe in check). I cannot resist the rigor of classicism, though I also need it combined with some theater. Formality is the warp, while fun flourishes are the weft that make up the tapestry I sought to weave in the design of the new living room.

Before any decorating could commence, I needed to make the living room symmetrical, so after we fabricated the false bookcase that came in from the dining room, we constructed its mate on the other side of the fireplace. While these bookcases are not symmetrically located on the walls they inhabit, they are in their relationship to the room's center. This placement was dictated by the tunneled space into the dining room, so in that regard, all I had to do was follow the math that resulted from that condition. The mantel also needed to be replaced; as it happened, one that I designed for Chesneys worked perfectly for the space. With symmetry established, the focal naturally became the fireplace, as is so often the case, and the dramatically crisp-white marble mantel against a "black absolute" marble chimney surround serves as a happy exclamation mark.

Sitting opposite the fireplace is an extra-long, extra-deep, luxuriously comfortable linen-upholstered sofa with Givenchy's inset tape trim application and finished with coral and red tassels at its skirt (for more on Givenchy, see page 225). To balance out the ratio between skirted pieces, leggy chairs, and neutral tones to bursts of color, I kept the twin linen chairs from the apartment's first living room from 10E. These bergères au chapeau de gendarmes live on either side of the fireplace, while a red klismos and a purple bergère face off at either end of the sofa—in effect, separating the swaths of pale linen on each side of the room. Another fun seating option between the beige chairs is a bench that I made as a gift for Pavlos. Reminiscent of a fender bench, it fits two people comfortably, with its H-shaped top (for

Hampton) and legs made in the shape of a pi symbol (π) for Pavlos Papageorgiou.

While seating is a primary concern in a living room, what really makes this space sing for me are the collections and artwork throughout. The eye happily travels from tablescapes to high and low pieces working together. The tabletop collections are composed mostly of all-natural neutrals, and the only time you see color is in the marble specimens, which don't read as color to me, per se, because they are an organic phenomenon. I have an obvious soft spot for friezes and medallions in plaster, alabaster, and basalt. I love the strict monotones. I've never met a tazza I didn't want. And I love obelisks for so many reasons, chief among them is the height they lend to tablescapes.

The Massimo Listri photograph of the Vatican's Sala delle Muse in the Museo Pío Clementino hangs above the sofa in the predominantly off-white color scheme of the living room. Some people hang portraits of their ancestors in their houses, but I prefer portraits of beautiful rooms and places for posterity. I also love how the items in the photo complement the actual friezes, busts, and sculptures in the room, and even the square panes of my casement windows—truly an instance where art imitates life (or life imitates art that imitates life?). The same meta quality is in the opposing wall with the photograph by Celia Rogge of busts displayed in Munich Residenz. Gilded plaster medallions of Roman emperors are mounted in the recessed area abutting the fireplace. I hung smaller bas-relief Caesars under the hot-pink lampshades, which hit at an extremely satisfying level when one is seated. Displaying artwork at a lower register creates a rhythm that keeps the eye from falling into a static state.

While the bevy of classical elements in the room could be read as formal, I think there are many fun flourishes throughout, such as the feathered helmets, which, I hope, communicate that I don't take my collections too seriously. This definitely isn't one of those

---

OPPOSITE: In this predominantly neutral living room, bursts of color come through in the artwork, the upholstery in the bergère, and the coffee table, lamps, and wainscoting.

TOP: As I moved through this current phase of embellishment, I added decorative interest to the brown Givenchy-esque slipper chairs and added various other frills to detail the room more thoroughly.

ABOVE: I designed this fender bench, which incorporates our initials, for Pavlos in 2015.

LEFT: Celia Rogge's incredible photography hangs above the living room fireplace and is also seen throughout the pages of this book (see pages 165 to 171, 147 to 155, and 121 to 127).

too-precious rooms that no one ever uses. In fact, you can often find me sitting on the Irish-matting-covered floor with my back leaning against the sofa working (or scrolling Instagram for the next architectural model to acquire). Overall, I'm really happy there is a good mix of casual and comfortable components (the most casual element of all is me wearing a concert T-shirt and my husband's boxer shorts) to balance out the more extravagant imperial decorative moments. What can I do? The heart loves what the heart loves.

ABOVE: I've tried to move away from the days when I framed my own paintings. Eventually, I was embarrassed by the amateurishness of my own handiwork. A massive Massimo Listri photograph has pride of placement in the living room above the sofa.

LEFT: Specimen-marble samples known as *pietra dura* were an oft collected souvenir of the grand tour.

OPPOSITE: When seated in this bergère, I can't help but see either the feathered helmet or the candlesticks decorated with miniature shields, axes, and maces, I am reminded of a time and place where beauty in public settings was a baseline. The virtuosity of the craftsmanship in a hat for someone putting out a fire is a total folly, yet also undeniably romantic.

ABOVE: After I outgrew a homemade painting I did of a segment of the Parthenon frieze, I hung a magnificent photo of the Greek Gallery by Celia Rogge, a friend and fine-art photographer. It remained there until I added the current Massimo Listri photograph, which shows the Vatican's Sala delle Muse and offered much needed color to this wall.

LEFT: The astrological symbols for the five members of my immediate family appear on the ceiling of the living room. Here we see Gemini and Taurus depicted to represent Pavlos and me.

OPPOSITE: In addition to the ones I have displayed in my home, believe it or not, I have several more specimen-marble collections in my office. The ones in the office are made up of twelve different varieties of marble in one-inch increments, which I use as rulers, imbuing the more quotidian aspects of my work with a flair of undeniable romance.

THIS PAGE, CLOCKWISE FROM TOP LEFT: By hanging the little Caesar plasters under the lamps, I have my Givenchy moment because I am reminded of his rooms where items can be found at a lower register so that they are eye level when a person is seated.

I love how the russet tones are repeated throughout my mostly neutral living room, especially in the trompe l'oeil porphyry background of Ashley Hicks's paintings hung near the entrance. When I commissioned these paintings, Ashley immediately suggested porphyry, and he was so right!

Having two of Ashley's paintings meant that I could hang one on each side of the stairs with complementary tablescapes on the temple bookcases underneath. Hicks and Hampton meet again.

OPPOSITE: These fake book spines pivot close and lay flat to appear as real when opened to transit from the living room to the dining room—they create a book-lined tunnel.

THE ROOM THAT KEEPS ON GIVING

Our family room is one of the original rooms from the first apartment that Pavlos and I had. As such, it has undergone a few incarnations. The updates generally involve the artwork displayed and the color scheme. The furniture plan devised so long ago in 2000 remains largely unchanged, I'm proud to say. When it was the living room, it boasted cool sandy tones. In its new iteration as a family room, I chose Farrow & Ball Oval Room Blue.

When it came time to decorate my own home as it stands today, I diverged a bit from my normal process with clients, where the plans for the interior decoration frequently precede the final purchasing or assembly of all the art. In my apartment, I obviously had extensive knowledge of what artwork I owned, which informed many of my choices as things came together. I drew and redrew the compositions of my collections, which were not necessarily pedigreed but deeply personal, as I wanted to make sure my choices reflected Pavlos's and my tastes exactly, and authentically—the incorporation of fantasy notwithstanding. Where the artwork is monotone, I often prefer colored walls (dining room and family room); where it is vibrant, I like a more settled palette (living room). Occasionally, when the artwork is in a certain color range, I like to use its opposite number (the complementary hue on the color wheel) on the walls (the purple bedroom with its bright green landscapes). No matter what the color setting, I feel that there is an absolute intimacy in what is hanging on our walls and that we have shared what those pictures say about us directly with our kids, including and encompassing them in the narrative as well. These are just some lessons that my heroes have demonstrated to me.

Did someone say "lesson?" Settle in, folks—here's a story about a time I experienced how meaningfully artwork can function in public versus private spaces. Shortly after starting to work at my father's firm full-time at the age of twenty-two, I accompanied him on a trip to Paris where he was decorating the American Embassy. He was working for the wickedly smart Pamela Harriman, a woman of incredible accomplishment whom I feel often does not get her due, when she was appointed ambassador to France in 1993 under President Bill Clinton. I think my father saw this as a graduation trip for me, and it certainly felt like a gift. And, even though I was surely more of a hassle than a helper to him, that visit proved to be a wonderfully formative experience for me. For example, I learned then that I was allergic to dust, but that was by no means the only discovery I would make.

For starters, that was the first time I ever really focused on the painter Paul César Helleu, whom I now adore. To see how Ambassador Harriman's collection of that single artist fomented into an entire decorating vibe was, to me, a revelation. She had an incredible art collection that included Picasso (love), Renoir (detest), Matisse (a favorite), Seurat (okay), Sargent (a favorite), and Calder (sure), and she had generously sprinkled many of them on loan throughout the embassy, upping its already considerable game several notches. However, in her private quarters, she had sited her collection of Helleu paintings, pieces perhaps less revered among historians but clearly more personal to her. Their subjects were almost always, if not exclusively, focused on a single figure of a single woman in a personal space. And there the ambassador was—a single and singular woman in an exceptional post.

At that moment, although I have always understood how critical a role artwork plays in life and in interior design, I really appreciated the autobiographical value it could lend an interior while also enriching the overall beauty of the space and effectively delineating public versus private places. These depictions of intimate subjects decidedly belonged to her and her alone. She could have had anything, but these drawings and paintings made her happy, and she kept them close and out of the public display, like the women themselves who were portrayed, often busy in their boudoirs.

The narrative of my father's and Harriman's decorating choices was both legible and coherent. It was undeniable that the apartment's occupant was in Paris, in an embassy setting with its wonderful French artwork and French boiserie and French painting styles (I once saw painters dragging hunks of wax down the walls to create a textured strié—wow!). The glamor of that storied house,

OPPOSITE: The custom green shade that I used on this porcelain lamp was just the thing in 2014. But by 2015, it needed to be made in purple silk and lined with crimson.

What is a family room without a television? Don't worry, it's there below all the books in the Napoleon III bookcase, hidden from view when not in service.

itself designed for an American woman in Paris, was beyond seductive. To be cozily dining with the ambassador and my father in her study, using our finger bowls (admittedly less cozy, and somewhat stressful), felt very special, not unlike being Gigi in the movie of the same name. Only, in this case, of course, my father wasn't my grandmother/pimp, nor was I an underaged courtesan in training. (Seriously, how did I not pick up on that plot point when I was younger?! *This* was considered MGM family fare? Harrumph.)

ABOVE: Our family has grown to five (seven if you count our sweet dogs, Percy and Athena) since Pavlos and I first stepped foot into this room. Here is how it looked in 2015, shortly after the renovations were completed.

LEFT: An incredible black-lacquered Empire bookcase is topped by other black figurines, tazzas, straight edges, and an Athenian helmet.

OPPOSITE: Like the fusion in our foods, it would be difficult to define hard-and-fast rules as to what makes up traditional American design. But one thing is sure, the best examples have a deft touch. While I may be exuberant about my helmets, I use them in strict compositions.

CABANA

TOP: A black granite tabletop provides a nice contrast to the natural colors of the marble specimens and metal lions.

ABOVE: A swag-and-jabot valance with a fuchsia tassel trim dresses the windows just so without obscuring any light.

RIGHT: This is the opposite end of the color story from my living room where the majority of the furniture is neutral and the artwork is more vibrant. Here I employ vibrant upholstery in the furniture while the artwork is predominantly monochromatic.

OPPOSITE: Any distinguishing architectural details, such as the Charles X marble fireplace, had to be brought in because the building itself was lacking. I love the graceful scrolls on the fireplace so much, I re-created it for my mantel collection at Chesney's.

ABOVE: Updating the sofa with a richly textured red velvet and tasseled trim was the perfect exclamation point to the family room's color story that also features lively paisley prints (on the chair and handmade lampshade by Marian McEvoy).

HOUSE BEAUTIFUL, SOUL BEAUTIFUL

Fashion designers and interior designers seemingly share a twin-flame connection, swirling around each other's orbit, which makes a good argument for the line of thought that says one's house is an extension of its inhabitants, much like the body is the vessel for the soul. A favorite book of mine, *The Fashion House*, takes a look at the interiors of some beloved fashion designers. In the book's introduction, the author writes, "I have always been fascinated by the concept of the creative whole, the entire artist. Perhaps I'm irrevocably condemned to a lifetime of frivolous thought." I took umbrage at that notion. There is nothing frivolous about the house in which you live! And I don't think the book's author, Lisa Lovatt-Smith, actually believes that either. Her book is just too good!

For as long as humans have walked the earth, we've been sketching our dreams and decorating our dwellings, whether permanent or not. I won't be so bold as to suggest a reason why that compulsion to beautify our surroundings or express ourselves through art is germane to our humanity but, as a professional in the field of interior design, I can attest to its impact. The scientific research on how hospital patients in a room with a view require less pain medication and fewer days in post-op than their counterparts in a windowless room seems obvious to me because having beauty in our lives is very healing and sustaining.

Which brings me to how we all must decorate the rooms of our kids. Children, too, deserve to be surrounded by beauty. Beauty is every bit as foundational for them as it is for adults. However, given that our offspring can express some of what they like does not always mean that they know how to achieve it. So, I like to use a Jedi mind trick when decorating for my children (I'm much more generous with other people's children, naturally). I ask my kids one or two major questions, like *What is your favorite color?* Or, *Would you like a bunk bed or a canopy bed?* Then I take it from there with that very meaningful but extremely limited input.

This is how my daughter ended up in a handsome neoclassical reverie of two-tone avocado walls. It has a green-plaid wool-covered bed inset in a niche, surrounded by framed friezes in shadow boxes lined with brown linen and set in golden egg-and-dart frames. On the background of the green suede panels sits an almost trompe l'oeil, perspective-expanding Massimo Listri photograph of the dining room of the Genoese Palazzo Tursi. Kiki's bedroom is the room of an aged adult, but everyone tells her how beautiful it is, and I say that she decorated it. She feels a huge amount of pride, and, for a long time, she has bought into it. Having said that, I definitely took advantage of her good nature. While our actual guest room is amazing, it has only a twin bed. So, when Pavlos's parents visit—and that is always for a minimum of a month—she gets displaced into the guest bedroom, and we rotate her queen bed out of the niche for them to use. Octogenarians and nonagenarians don't need as much floor space to play, they say. So, I was decorating not just for Kiki, but for our grown-up visitors and me.

When Kiki first moved into the room, she was six. In her early teens now, she has removed the friezes and plastered the room with actual vinyl records, a guitar, and band posters that she lovingly tapes to the wall just so, and everywhere the eye can see. I have recently offered her carte blanche to redecorate, feeling that I owe her for her years of friendly acquiescence. So far, she has demurred, saying that, while she no longer favors green, she does love it in that room and she'll keep it, the bed, and the Listri. As long as I let her have the surrounding walls, she's good.

And now, I am holding my breath.

OPPOSITE: With my love of an alcove bedroom (I'm talking to you, *Neoclassicism of the North*), I had to create one for my daughter. Hanging on suede squares with stitched corners is yet another Massimo Listri photograph. We frequently "requisition" this room for visiting couples (read: my in-laws), so the room's tenor has always exceeded my daughter in maturity.

ABOVE: In order to make Kiki's room bigger, we stole real estate from the guest room. While it began its life small, it is now positively diminutive in size. I decorated it with as much ambition as any other room, turning it into a jewelbox replete with gallery walls of artwork, pretty much every blessed piece of wall is covered.

LEFT: An earlier incarnation of the tiny guest room shows the Louis XVI daybed frame in blue-and-white upholstery.

OPPOSITE: This small corner of the teeny-weeny guest bedroom shows two framed metal busts, a watercolor that I painted of Bill Blass's living room, and, above the lampshade, a beautiful woven photo by the late, great Fernando Bengoechea. His brother now keeps his memory alive by painstakingly re-creating his work.

GROWING CONFIDENCE WITH USING COLOR IN MY ABODE

The most exciting dimensional element of the new principal bedroom would be the addition of coffers to the ceiling, which Hyde Park Mouldings made for me. Each coffer contains a central classical medallion and is further punctuated by the addition of plaster egg-and-dart molding to really turn up the lushly luxurious quotient of the room. To ground the opulence of the coffers, I had a ticking stripe wallpaper applied to the background behind the medallions. I find this addition brings a casual elegance to that otherwise formal feature (I was thinking of Sweden at the time). I really love those medallions, though my husband can't help himself from referring to them as "radishes."

Initially, I carried over the same neutral color palette in the new principal bedroom as it had been before the renovation in an effort to reuse the elements that had worked so successfully before. But after Pavlos and I lived in it for a few months, I realized it just didn't translate well in the new room. This is what we now refer to as the Great Bedroom Debacle of 2015 (see page 220). Our new bedroom's diminutive size and lack of wall-spanning bookcases required a bold use of color to bring up the energy of the space. While pretty, it felt somehow ordinarily so. There was nothing to signal that it was the head bedroom, perched atop the hierarchy of all the bedrooms.

I went on a soul-searching mission to find a color that would speak to what I wanted to achieve in that room and found myself back in the daydreams of my youth. For as long as I can remember, I felt a very strong gravitational pull to the color purple. I was drawn to its vibrancy and ineffable emotional tug. Of all the colors in the rainbow, though, purple tends to be the most polarizing (see page 81 for why I eschewed decorating with it for years). As a child, I didn't pick up on the associations the color has with royalty, creativity, and mysticism. I didn't know that violet's electromagnetic wavelength is so strong that it sits next to X-rays and gamma rays in the light spectrum. All I knew was that I liked it and wanted to be dressed head to toe in it. And then, perhaps, seeing David Hicks's bedroom at the Albany imprinted upon me what an ideal bedroom ought to be.

The purple-and-orange combination that came into view for the color scheme is nothing I'd ever lived with, but I love it so much. Knowing the amplifying impact of dark walls in small spaces, I covered the walls with a custom-colored, Gracie block-patterned wallpaper that has the appearance of suede. I switched out the bed curtains with a silk paisley and trimmed it all with a gold laurel-leaf trim (which has since been partially devastated by my dog's teeth when he was a puppy). The exterior of the canopy is purple cotton velvet, sumptuous to the touch and an extension of sorts to the texture of the wall treatment. The mirror-embroidered bedspread was a textile that I found on Etsy, and I backed it with a Fortuny fabric because I am just so extra (or pretend to be). The rug underneath the bed is Turkish Oushak; it, in turn, is layered over a graphic, Hicks-inspired design by me and made by Crosby Street Studios. There is a lot of *a lot* going on in this room. But, I promise you, the effect is harmonious.

On some level, I believe people get into the business of interior design because they like to please people. Essential work it is not, but it does provide a necessary outlet for me to express this need I have to help people create beautiful surroundings. With this bedroom, I felt I had come full circle creating something for myself and Pavlos that I absolutely loved, now that I have grown older and more confident in knowing what pleases me, and, as it happens, what pleases him.

OPPOSITE: From suede wallpaper and velvet bed curtains to layered rugs and bedspreads, plush textures and rich colors abound in my sleeping quarters, yet they never prove disquieting.

This vanilla color scheme worked beautifully in our last bedroom (see page 139) because of the large size and grand dimensions, but the palette did not translate well in the new space and is henceforth known as the Great Bedroom Debacle of 2015. It was such a rookie mistake (and expensive). But the current design as it stands now (see previous pages) was worth all the headache.

The antelope carpet from STARK has always been a favorite carpet and brought enough interest in the dressing room to anchor it.

I thought my million-dollar idea was hiding the television behind a painting on an easel. I was disabused of that notion after my friend told me Restoration Hardware had been selling such things for years. Oh well, back to the drawing board. At least while I am dreaming up ideas, I can look west and north over the city's buildings.

ABOVE: The 1960s porcelain faux bois lamps on the bedside tables were originally in the living room but work better here with the French nightstands that I found at auction.

RIGHT: Amethyst is said to imbue spaces with healing and calming qualities. Who knows, but it certainly can't hurt. Here, I bought a slab and swapped out the prior anodyne tabletops. I still can't believe I had the gall!

OPPOSITE, CLOCKWISE FROM TOP: While I am tempted to futz with my bedroom, it truly needs to remain static. It is a small room that already looks great. But then a painting with the perfect colors will cross my path, and the next thing I know, I've found a spot for it above the headboard. Here is Pierre Bergian's interior portrait of a room at Carlos de Beistegui's Groussay, another inspiration for all time. And so it goes.

Red, orange, pink, and purple—once I abandoned my white-and-taupe scheme, I really let go.

Little corded closures, called frogs, bedecked my bed's canopy. No detail went missing in this room.

METAMORPHOSIS

As any butterfly could tell you if they spoke, transformations can be very messy and, at times, somewhat painful. For the caterpillar to ditch its earthbound form and emerge into a winged beauty, its insides must melt into a goo, during which time its cells reorganize themselves in its chrysalis. While this analogy may sound dramatic, it is fitting for what is to come through the different iterations of our house. The renovations themselves took the time needed to be done right, just as a broken bone needs time to set and heal—as we learned when Markos broke his foot and Kiki broke both of her wrists and then one of her wrists for the second time (no doubt, the emergency-room doctor was starting to give us funny looks).

I won't bore you, dear reader, with the travails of this renovation (and there were many because we lived in the apartment during them), but I do want to share one nugget of gold. The secret to a good renovation is the same as the secret to being a good parent: Patience.

ABOVE, LEFT: I love white kitchens, I love colored kitchens, and I love black kitchens. This one, which has Fornasetti plates hanging on the wall and a Piranesi at the entrance, is as decorated as the rest of the apartment.

ABOVE, RIGHT: The bar also boasts black and bamboo and is so handsome because of that. We have a second ice-machine here; that is the ultimate luxury!

OPPOSITE: A moody little breakfast bar built for three. As François & Co. advised, my custom-detailed pewter countertop was a great choice of materials, unlike zinc, which they described as a wild animal. Who knew?

HUBERT DE GIVENCHY

Before 1993, I knew of Givenchy exclusively as one of the great living fashion designers. Any American woman worth her salt was first a young girl who had an obsession with Audrey Hepburn—*Roman Holiday* with Gregory Peck, *Love in the Afternoon* with Gary Cooper, *Sabrina* with William Holden and Humphrey Bogart, *Breakfast at Tiffany's* with George Peppard (though I never got him, but Holly Golightly's hair and clothes more than made up for his being a bit of a dud), and, of course, *Charade* with Cary Grant. Givenchy and Hepburn had a famous friendship that led to an endless stream of flawless, love-powered fashion collaborations between savant and muse. The one-two punch of Audrey's gamine glow, radiant with its aura of sweetness, made sophisticated through Givenchy's incredible geometries and elegant fabrics was the perfect mix for an unmatched outcome. So, there was that.

Then, boom. I, and everyone in the design world who didn't already know it, became acquainted with Le Style Givenchy when his first sale hit Christie's in 1993. I had just entered my twenties and can honestly say that it changed my appreciation of French design for all time. Of course, I'd seen amazing Parisian interiors. I have made multiple pilgrimages to the Musée Nissim de Camondo on the edge of the Parc Monceau. I have gratefully stayed in a mouthwatering apartment nestled among the mansard roofs overlooking the Place Vendôme. I painted an interior view of the entry of the Hôtel Lambert, which lived in my apartment for years. I went with my father when he decorated the American Embassy for Pamela Harriman and even lived in Versailles with a family one semester of my tenth-grade year, but . . . c'mon! The Givenchy sale landed with unparalleled impact. And, looking around the design community today, I can happily attest to the fact that I was not the only one so galvanized by this event.

The "Givenchy Sofa" with its inset tape trim, fringe, and wing arms entered the American design lexicon (and eventually my living room). Regal Givenchy

> "Every aspect of these rooms is designed, but they escape ever seeming labored over or overlabored."

green became synonymous with dignified elegance. The tree-of-life-enshrouded guest bedroom, with its lit à la polonaise anchored along a wall at the Le Jonchet, has even been lovingly re-created almost piece for piece many, many times over. These are just a few examples, and yet, for all the ubiquity of the Givenchy influence, his style never seems anything but timeless, whether authored by the man himself or by the many who revere him.

L'Hôtel d'Orrouer, built for a marquise of that name by architect Pierre Boscry, is my particular idea of perfection. With a facade of tailored austerity and adorned on its inside with panels gilded to just the right degree, Givenchy's luxurious interiors somehow achieved a kind of rigorousness that defied the presence of the occasional massive piece of Boulle furniture. It was also interesting to me for being, generally, a single color scheme unspooled through each room, again suggesting a methodical quality to Givenchy's approach to rich interiors. The overall effect of all the greens dotted with gold tones, which appear in the form of gold leaf, ormolu, and brass, was of a scrupulously handsome and harmonious, albeit opulent, series of rooms.

While he was known, I have been told, as having the best "sit furniture" in Paris, the rooms' various compositions are also unspeakably accomplished. These encompass every plane, from his arrangement of candelabra on the walls and his furniture placements to the objects on tables and the negative space in between those objects. Every aspect of these rooms is designed, but they escape ever seeming labored over or overlabored. They are interiors to be enjoyed all at once but then subsequently

---

OPPOSITE: Givenchy's green salon in his home at the Hôtel d'Orrouer in Paris will always be one of my favorite rooms. Its perfect symmetry brings together rococo and neoclassical styles into a perfect whole.

savored inch by inch. Perhaps this is not unlike his achievements in couture.

In 2022, so many years after that first sale, I was able to fly to Paris for one night so that I could see the second great Christie's Givenchy sale in person. For quite some time, I agonized over whether I should go, until I just accepted the fact that if I didn't, I would likely regret it forever. The magic of all his homes—including Le Clos Fiorentina in Saint-Jean-Cap-Ferrat, the manoir Le Jonchet in Romilly-sur-Aigre, and his hôtel particulier on the Rue de Grenelle, mentioned previously—will always inspire. For every piece of porphyry, there is a Giacometti sculpture or a faux-bone Parsons side table. For each tiger silk velvet is its opposite number, a ruffled white slipcover. He knew how to authentically embrace every

sides of the design spectrum. The one thing holding it all together was his unerring love of beauty. Givenchy's interiors are brilliant examples of expansive design influences working splendidly together when there is a solid through line. This singularly tall man cast a long shadow.

ABOVE, LEFT: Various tablescapes at Givenchy's L'Hôtel d'Orrouer show his devotion to exalting the most mundane objects alongside the most divine. Everything is placed in an almost inevitable position.

ABOVE RIGHT: The color story that Givenchy told through his clothing designs and home decor was layered and nuanced.

OPPOSITE: Symmetry, balance, beauty, and scale—everything in Givenchy's homes is taken into consideration.

OPPOSITE: Amid the grandeur that is intrinsic to the Hôtel d'Orrouer, it was built for a marquis after all, Givenchy designed a uniquely comfortable living room where slipcovered furniture is gathered around Empire tables and telescoping drinks tables, all lit overhead by a Charles X chandelier.

ABOVE, LEFT: The graceful curves of this Empire bronze vase are matched by the Empire commode upon which it rests.

ABOVE, RIGHT: Green was clearly Givenchy's favorite color, and he used it to great effect throughout his home. It is now known as "Givenchy Green" to his many disciples.

ABOVE: This bedroom, with ceilings as high as the green salon's, has a lighter touch of Givenchy's green, but the elegance and glamor ring through and through.

FAR LEFT: Givenchy's wealth of textile knowledge from fashion spilled over into his interior decor. Here, shades of green appear in the frog enclosures and fringe decorating a skirted table.

LEFT: Givenchy's mastery of grand embellishment is matched by his occasional restraint. Here a bird's-eye view of two dishes on a tabletop seems as beautiful to me as any Vermeer painting.

OPPOSITE: The clean lines of the canopy play off the lines of the gilt box molding trim, while the curves of the gilding of the ceiling molding play off the embroidery on the bed quilt.

2014 KIPS BAY SHOW HOUSE: MARRAKECH ME IF YOU CAN

Decorating the landmark Villard House for the 2014 Kips Bay Decorator Show House might possibly be one of my favorite Kips Bay experiences, which is saying a lot considering how much I love every aspect of working with these show houses. Built in the early 1880s on Madison Avenue in New York City, the McKim, Mead & White–designed Villard House with its sixteen-foot-tall ceilings is simply stunning. Offered an envelope that amazing, I knew I had to pull out all the stops.

When I was invited to participate, I remembered that my last room in 2012 was a very glossy, very sexy monochromatic bedroom (see pages 157 to 163), so I knew this time I could do neither a bedroom nor a subdued palette. I had to do the theoretical opposite, so I set my sights on a living room and ruled out a uniform color scheme in favor of elaborate patterns. I drew inspiration from one of the seminal rooms I encountered in my teen years in the Mudéjar triumph that is the Casa de Pilatos in Seville, Spain.

After doing a deep dive to find tile patterns I liked, I somehow narrowed it down to two. I knew my palette would be extreme: purples, greens, reds, rubies, navy, and gold. I worked with Chuck Fischer to custom-color the large main-tile design, which was then repeated to create a digitally printed wallpaper. The purple, blues, and greens that we chose for the design would then be echoed throughout the room's fabric scheme. I knew the stiles and rails had to be green, which goes with everything because it's the color of nature. The lower tile pattern was reproduced exactly as I found it in an inspirational photograph. I love how small, busy patterns can function like a solid color in an overall design scheme.

Once I had the tile pattern and the colors figured out, I pulled fabrics: cut velvet, ikats, stripes, paisleys, checks, *everything*. I sketched out the room and then gathered furniture from numerous sources. The hallmark for many decorators working on show houses is simplicity because it's hard to layer during such a short time, but

> "I love how small, busy patterns can function like a solid color in an overall design scheme."

this room was so large that we needed to throw as much as we could at it, hence going so far as adding a birdcage, which was in that first concept drawing, and eventually even a mother-of-pearl elephant in the fireplace.

The art came last, and I got enormously lucky finding a series of large-format paintings that looked as though they had been made for the room. The incredible abstract work is from Franklin Tartaglione, who, in addition to fine art painting, is also a much-in-demand decorative painter with whom my firm has had the great privilege of working for decades. My stalking of Massimo Listri also paid off and I was able to hang, above one of the many seating areas, one of his photographs of the Tuscan-Moorish revival extravaganza that is Castle Sammezzano. Above the corner banquette, I hung a gallery of much smaller works, including some by the late Julian Barrow (whom I also collect), which I hoped might allow people to see how a real person might create a scaled-down, cozy area in such a room. Any good collection, especially of art, is acquired over time during which one's interest evolves; the result frequently consists of various-size pieces. Unlike large-format works in such a big room, small paintings don't readily lend themselves to obvious placement—love can be messy at times. Here, I think we demonstrated well how it might be done to good effect. You treat the whole of them as a single large array and use it in relation to the larger-scale works. I added Irish matting as a floor covering because it was a great foil for everything else and I wanted to balance the Mudéjar

OPPOSITE, TOP: All the jewel tones and rich textures in the room somehow suggest to me the deep layers of a rich tagine. I know I'm onto something if it seems delicious.

OPPOSITE, BOTTOM: Having several intimate seating options makes a room this large feel cozy and expansive at once. It's such a luxury to have such space, and it demands proper handling

Massimo Listri's photograph of the Castle Sammezzano, a Tuscan-Moorish revival masterpiece with its rich textures, serves as a monochrome tonic to the wildly colored tile wallpaper.

ABOVE, TOP TO BOTTOM: Just as convex bullseye mirrors are a telltale sign of John Soane, lions are my mark (and coincidentally, St. Mark is always shown with his lion).

If you're paying attention closely, you might recognize the purple lamps from my own family room.

A mother-of-pearl-inlaid table offers another opportunity for pattern texture and a glistening additional material.

ABOVE: I had never done this type of window treatment before, or since, though not for lack of desire! To pull it off successfully required a really big window and a whole lot of moxie.

elements, which would prevent me from descending into a kitschy theme room with the potential to be characterized as Alexa's Casbah.

The grand finale was the Chinese lanterns that were purchased in Manhattan's Chinatown for less than twenty dollars each. They were the right colors and solved my aversion to chandeliers in living rooms. I loved that they didn't detract from the central focal point of the desk, which worked as the room's organizing principle. Besides, the lanterns were just so much more fun and unexpected, much like my goal for this Kips Bay room itself.

The Moroccan room marked an exciting time in my life when I was feeling confident enough to stray away from what I had been doing in the recent past and by quite a large amount. I didn't set out an intention to change people's opinion of me, but rather expand it while having a ton of fun simply creating and playing

with color in a bold way. I am still so happy and proud of this room because I loved how it all came together, and, as an added bonus, it ushered in new and different commissions for the firm.

ABOVE: I tried to gather all the books authored by my fellow designers in the show house. Show houses are community events, after all, and we feel connected when we participate in them together.

OPPOSITE, TOP TO BOTTOM: If you took a drink every time you saw one of my own pieces of furniture in a show house that I designed, you'd be in trouble. The coral klismos is a repeat offender.

The fifty shades of green in this little tableau really do drive home the fact that green does go with everything—from the fiddle-leaf fig tree and orchid leaves to the marble tabletop and textured velvet chaise longue.

2018 KIPS BAY SHOW HOUSE: OLYMPIA'S FOLLY

At the 2018 Kips Bay Decorator Show House, I fully committed myself to going deep into a genre in a fun and fantastical way, much like I live in real life with my feathered helmets. By 2018, I had hit my stride with bold uses of color—as exemplified by the 2014 Kips Bay room and my own purple bedroom—so I wanted to give myself a different challenge. My idea of keeping things fresh meant I would go back to the classics thematically and see how far I could take trompe l'oeil.

Trompe l'oeil fell out of favor after we all loved it too much in the 1980s, and its ubiquity dulled our taste for it. When done well, however, it is a display of expert artistry, much in the same way that parquetry is featured in the Met's Studiolo from the Ducal Palace or in the adroit designs done currently by Studio Peregalli. When I look at Studio Peregalli's body of work, I know their clients can afford to do anything, yet they have decided to celebrate the virtuosity of the faux, which is such a refreshing celebration of what artisans can do. I applaud as well as admire it.

I wanted to celebrate this type of masterful craftsmanship for my room, so I cold-called storied handprinted wallpaper company de Gournay to ask if they would like to collaborate with me. I was over the moon when they agreed to create the swagged wallpaper I envisioned and then further agreed to a wall of a scenic landscape as well. And, of course, once again, I had to enlist Chuck Fischer, who helped me create the tiled wallpaper in the Moroccan Room in 2014 (see pages 233 to 239).

This time, Chuck played a major role in structuring the elevations and engineering my design for the fabric curtains to work with the painted ones on the walls and the ceiling. He also executed the original artwork for the idealized Greek landscape viewed from the "tent," based on a small black-and-white print that I had in my office.

> "My idea of keeping things fresh meant I would go back to the classics thematically and see how far I could take trompe l'oeil."

I cannot overstate how crucial Chuck was in the engineering of this feat. From one little drawing, he was able to pull the vision I had in my head for the perfect view of the space I wanted to create, scaling it properly, correcting the perspective, and placing objects in the foreground to relate properly to the opening of the curtains and what was displayed beyond the tent.

All told, the effort created the illusion of a tented space, reminiscent of an imperial campaign tent during the Roman Empire, overlooking an idealized ancient town. There were three different productions happening simultaneously across the world: The draped wallpaper was hand-painted in China; with the logistics of its creation directed by de Gournay in London; while in New York, the furniture and curtains were made locally, and Chuck hand-painted the ceiling. They all joyously came together on a wing and a prayer (minus the day I spent anxious and crying in a bathroom at the show house). The only real draping in that room is at the windows. I loved watching people's expressions the moment they realized there wasn't actually fabric on the walls or ceiling. There was a lot of touching the walls in disbelief.

Once the Mongiardino-inspired stagecraft of creating the draped wallpaper and ceiling was underway, I got to work pulling together furniture via the long-honored tradition of show-house decorating: beg or borrow (or steal—wink-wink). Doris Leslie Blau lent us the gorgeous, colorful Khorassan rug, which worked so perfectly with all the furniture. The beautiful upholstered sofa and curtains came from Anthony

OPPOSITE: The mix of dark wood furniture and a porphyry timepiece is fit for royalty.

I tip my hat to Mongiardino with trompe l'œil walls, and Soane with convex bullseye mirrors.

Lawrence-Belfair, with whom my firm has worked for more than four decades. Newel Antiques was kind enough to loan me the Russian secretary and table, which was a boon because Russian furniture has always been a particular favorite of mine. The paisley chairs we covered were so good that I just had to purchase them from 145 Antiques, one of my favorite sources for antique upholstery. And speaking of home, the coral klismos chair, coffee table, feathered helmet, and low temple bookcases were taken straight out of my own living room. There is very little I wouldn't sacrifice for the Kips Bay cause (my husband has since forbidden this practice).

As is often the case when working with clients, the artwork was the last layer. Hanging above the velvet sofa is a photograph of the Munich Residenz, which used to house Bavarian royalty, taken by Celia Rogge, my dear friend, fine art photographer, and frequent collaborator.

A crop of that photograph hangs above my own living room mantel, which, along with the purchase of the paisley chairs, represents one of the many hazards of my profession. Sometimes I just can't let go of something I've used in a different context and I wind up taking it home with me. Thank GOD, my current contribution to the Kips Bay Boys and Girls Club is serving as the Show House co-chair, keeping me slightly less in the path of temptation for the moment.

ABOVE: As the entrance to this room precluded the placement of too much furniture, I substituted it with a fantasy landscape, devised by Chuck Fischer and realized by de Gournay. As I told the *New York Times,* I've clearly seen *Gladiator* one too many times.

OPPOSITE: By the time I was decorating this room, I had already re-decorated my bedroom into the orange-and-purple confection that it is currently, so I would say I fully hit my stride using colors with abandon.

OPPOSITE, TOP TO BOTTOM: I wish I could say decorating this room helped ease my obsession with neoclassicist design; instead, it has only fortified it.

The river flows both ways when it comes to which of my own personal items are used to decorate a show house and which pieces I've borrowed for a show house come back home with me afterward. The white neoclassical bookcases were mine before the show, and the paisley chairs were mine after the show house closed.

ABOVE: Givenchy green makes an appearance in the curtain tassels and lamp as a nod to the master of what he called "noble simplicity." Also, take another sip of your cocktail, because there's the hardest working chair I own: my coral klismos.

RECONCILING INFLUENCES

With my background, I appreciate traditional design because I think it's harder. You have to have such a deep relationship with what is on display and an understanding of how pieces interact with one another on an almost molecular level. It would be much easier to fill one's house with all square-edged sofas and chairs à la Jean-Michel Frank—though, make no mistake, he was a genius and a pioneer. Minimalist design is eye-catching and eye-pleasing and can be simply divine, but obviously that's not what I'm trying to do here in my home.

I often think of different decorating preferences as the result of where we hop on if we were to envision the history of design as a merry-go-round. First, we get our seats; then, as it turns, our tastes shift as we go through life. For example, when David Hicks was born in 1929, he got on the design merry-go-round at a very traditional moment in English decor and then went on to define a type of 1960s modernism. In my case, I was born in the 1970s to a Technicolor plastic–loving world; so, in reaction to that, I very much love traditional design (as evidenced in 7G). But then I pared down and became a cleaner traditional for 10E + 10D's combination. Now I've gone further and become totally colorful and embellished again (or maybe just dizzy from all that spinning)—with the through line of neoclassicism because I find so much comfort in its solidity. Maybe I'll go back to plastic everything when I'm in my sixties or seventies. Who knows? As Greek philosopher Democritus said, "Nothing exists except atoms and empty space; everything else is opinion."

As mentioned earlier, my inspirations, though they are what they are, don't always show up in my rooms. This is for many reasons: space, budget, functionality, an understanding of how to incorporate things and where to do so, and designing rooms in certain geographical locations, even. For example, my family does not have its own country house, and my choices for the city are the result of its urban setting. But you had better believe that I'm going to keep striving and hoping to surround myself and my family with the results of all this lifelong input. One day, I would even love to report back with a book about a modern, or at least streamlined, country house. Stay tuned.

ABOVE: As I've entered into my fifth decade, my chickens are coming home to roost. These chickens are my love of robust patterns, Empire flourishes, and monumental photography and a desire to create celebratory interiors.

OPPOSITE, TOP: My latest published show house demonstrates many of my influences. They pop up in color, richness of pattern, selection of lines of furniture, the embrace of abundance, and a real love of the past.

OPPOSITE, BOTTOM LEFT: Flanking a carved étagère, pedestals (inspired by ones owned by Bill Blass) hold ferns above, creating a floral "order." The furniture is formal enough to keep the animal-print walls tamed.

OPPOSITE, BOTTTOM RIGHT: Dark, light, dark, light; I hope the result is effortless, but I am greatly concerned with the placement of furniture or contrasting finishes and the rhythm they create as they play out in any given room.

ACKNOWLEDGMENTS

This book is a product of love. Writing it with Rosy Ngo, my co-author and so much more, was a wild and sometimes harrowing feat with so many ideas, inspirations, influences, Post-it notes filled with anecdotes, and fun tangents distilled by deadlines, plus a couple bouts of COVID (for me) and long COVID (for her). That you now hold it in your hands is a testament to the kinship that started a decade earlier when she edited my first book. I cannot say enough nice things to satisfy the strong Leo placements in her birth chart.

Steve Freihon, whose principal photography graces these pages, is a long-time collaborator and one of the most fun people on Earth. We laughed ourselves hoarse on every shoot, and during a hundred phone calls during the process of creating this book. Celia Rogge, whose photography also graces this book in abundance, is not only a great photographer, but also one of my closest friends and like a sister to me. She had no idea what she was signing on for when she agreed to help me with this project, as her work went far beyond supplying photos. She also hopped on planes to London and Seville, and into cars and trains around Berlin and Potsdam for me, and on and on. My gratitude is endless. Thank you!

But the photo credits do not stop there, not by a long shot. Marlo Gamora, Andrew Frasz, and Chris Delaney from Steve's Tungsten team were invaluable. Natalie Freihon and Bowie Freihon are due either thanks or apologies. I'm not sure which. Many other esteemed collaborators permitted me to use their incredible work. These include Arthur Elgort, Ashley Hicks, Thibault Jeanson, the late Fernando Bengoechea, Fritz Von der Schulenberg, Francis Hammond, Scott Frances, Jean de Bourbon, Jeff Hirsch, Emily Followill, and Gieves Anderson. Your work is truly divine, and this book couldn't have happened without it.

My mother, Darling Duane, and my Aunt Paula deserve thanks that extend beyond supporting this book. I thank them for providing so much inspiration, design and otherwise, my whole life.

Elizabeth Blitzer, whose title is PR agent/Publicist extraordinaire, is actually my life coach and business mentor, whether she acknowledges this or not. If you ever have the chance to work with her, seize it. The experience will change your life.

The team at Mark Hampton LLC deserves much more than my thanks. My colleagues over the years have handled everything for me. While I get the credit, these wonderful people have done it all behind the scenes and at the sites. I owe them thanks for growing up beside me, helping me keep my father's legacy alive, and inspiring me with their immense talents and tireless hard work. Their loyalty, decency, humor, and friendship have been the bedrock of my life and career these past twenty-five years. COVID and life have scattered us, but only physically. My heart is with them all, regardless of their current locations: Mee Pinheiro, Dip-Min Yuen, Sara Mullen, Kate Callahan, Hannah Laird, Katharine Trigg, Mary Eugenia Hunt, Devon Morten, LeeLee Duryea, Maggie Irvin, Pat O'Brien, Tigran Guylan, David Steffenhagen, Lucinda Sussman, and the late, great Louise Cursio.

Other professional partners and friends who have collaborated with me are also of vital importance—with special emphasis on those who built my home, the narrative center of this book—as well as many of my other projects. I may thank them here, but I thank heaven for them every other day as well. This is Johnny Donadic, Benjamin Fischer, Dariusz Nowak (and his hamster), Gene Abbazio, and Carlo Amato and his family.

Anthony Lawrence-Belfair Draperies is also a big part of my career and life. First, there is my brother from another mother, Joe Calagna. We have walked pretty much hand in hand these past twenty-five years. We've shared deaths, weddings, and births. And alongside his wife, Amy Calagna, and his late sister Lana, and his brother-in-law Mike Giambattista, there have been beautiful curtains and upholstery everywhere we go! And it all has been the result of the love and labor of Soula Pavlou, DeAnna Pavlou, Jackie Caputo, Uliana Parkhomei, Sandrina Nesturi, and Anna Giorno. Thank you!

A million hands touched and adorned my apartment, each of which added something unique and priceless. These MVP collaborators include the entire Gracie Family (with Jen being my main co-conspirator/sister), Carlos Solano and his team at Prelude Painting, Adrian Taylor and his team at Hyde Park Mouldings, Judith Prause and her team at Chesneys, Tony Mott and everyone at Crosby Street Studios, Stasie Rowley and the whole STARK Carpet family, artist Chuck Fischer, J.M. Shea Paper Hanging, the whole Kravet Family (and team), Andy Singer and Gale Singer and my family at Visual Comfort, Christian Toledo, Jimmy Gomiela and the entire Celebrity Moving team, my friends from the Nazmiyal Gallery, Greg Gurfein and Dean Barger. Penn & Fletcher, Twenty2, Victoria & Son, Objets Plus Antiques, Hildy Strasser at J. Pocker, Guy Regal, Newel Gallery, the Shade Store, Franklin Tartaglione, and Tom Preston also provided crucial help. Thank you.

And where would this book be without the targets of my love letters and the sources of so much of my hero worship? Nowhere. So, thank you to Susan, Carter (II and III), and Belle Burden for an entire lifetime of love and friendship and family. Thank you to the Hicks family for two generations of inspirational family members. Thank you to Niall Smith for tutoring so many of us in the New York design industry with your flawless eye. Thank you to Hyatt Bass and Samantha Bass for your friendship and support and a shared childhood filled with love. Thank you to Sotheby's for helping me acquire the photos of my beloved Bill Blass's apartment and house. Thank you to the Givenchy Family for allowing me to salute Monsieur H., who was such a shining light to so many, and to Christie's who helped facilitate so much. Thank you to the John Soane Museum for existing and for opening your doors to Celia with her camera, and likewise to the teams at the Casa de Pilatos in Seville and the Foundation for Prussian Houses and Gardens in Berlin and Brandenburg. Thank you, Hakan Groth, for writing your seminal, drool-worthy book, *Neoclassicism in the North*. Thanks must also go to the Kips Bay Boys and Girls Club, Jim Druckman, Nazira Handel,

Daniel Quintero, Bunny Williams, and Jamie Drake for the invaluable work they do for 10,000 kids in the Bronx, and for inviting the entire design community in to be a part of their vital endeavors.

A boundless thank-you also has to go to the design titans, of print and online, whose support has made every bit of difference in the survival and success of my career. I'm talking to you, Amy Astley, Alison Levasseur, Margaret Russell, Marian McEvoy, Dara Caponigro, D.J. Carey, Penelope Green, Stephen Drucker, Senga Mortimer, Newell Turner, Michael Boodro, Whitney Robinson, Asad Syrkett, Sophie Donelson, Jo Salz, Margo Shaw, and Mark Mayfield.

Thank you, from the bottom of my heart, to Bobby Liberman and Kristen Fischer for making a loving home for AH Inc and MH LLC for thirty years.

Rosy also wants and needs to thank her invaluable support team for keeping her afloat and contributing to the birth of this book. This includes Flo Vagnetti, Jessica and Nathaniel Goldblatt, Lucy Rorech, and Donald Cantillo. We'd also like to send a special shout-out to Isabell Whitepaw, Aurora and Tilly Blackheart, and Percival Aurelius Hampton-Papageorgiou and Athina Hampton-Papageorgiou who have established their cred as vital support animals.

At Clarkson Potter, I must thank our designer Jenny Davis, art director Mia Johnson, editorial assistant Darian Keels, production manager Kim Tyner, marketer Allison Renzulli, and publicist Katherine Tyler.

And, last, William Clark: this is all your fault. Thank you for being my agent and for gently nudging me for a decade to write this. It's an honor to be your client and friend. Likewise, thanks are due to Angelin Adams, my editor at Clarkson Potter who took this on and encouraged us all along on our long and winding road.